THE MEITEI SOCIETY
A Study on Traditional Life Circle Ceremonies

THE MEITEI SOCIETY

A Study on Traditional Life Circle Ceremonies

N. BIRACHANDRA SINGH

AKANSHA PUBLISHING HOUSE

NEW DELHI • GUWAHATI • VISAKHAPATNAM

AKANSHA PUBLISHING HOUSE
4649-B/21, Ansari Road
Daryaganj, New Delhi - 110 002
Phones: 011-23263193, 9811582779, 0943116718
Fax: 011-23263193
Email: ektabooks@yahoo.com

The Meitei Society: A Study of Traditional Life Circle Ceremonies

First Published 2006

Reprint 2023

ISBN 81-8370-0586

PRINTED IN INDIA
Published by M.P. Misra for Akansha Publishing House, New Delhi.

Contents

INTRODUCTION

The state of Manipur lies in the north eastern corner of India on the Indo-Burma border. Geographically the land can be divided into two parts viz. the valley and the hills. The valley having an altitude of 2500mts is surrounded by nine ranges of hills. The hills are inhabited by different tribes and the valley is exclusively occupied by the Meiteis. The valley with fine scene is very pleasant throughout the year. So Jawaharlal Nehru has rightly called Manipur the jewel of India and another writer, Constentine has called it the Paradise of the world. Just before the beginning of the present era, the valley was under water. Not only the valley itself, the whole land was once under a sea called Tethys. The local Puya also gives the same view.

In the geographical term, in the Mesozoic era (230-60 million years) there was a long, deep and narrow sea known as Tethys which originated from the Mediterranean Sea and extended toward the east occupying the northern boundary of India, including Manipur. In this geosyenline sea sediments were deposited throughout the ages and the depth of the sea was swallowing set by set. In the latest cretaceous (135-50 million years) erogenic activities led to the upliftment of the highland of Burma, Shan plateau including certain portion of Manipur hills.[1]

From the account of fossils available in Samdal in the eastern district of Manipur, the hills were formed in the cretaceous period (135-50 million years).[2] By the middle of the cretecous period the Tethyan Sea was withdrawn from this region by the great organic activities of the period.[3] The process of upliftment of the Himalayan range, Alps and its branches took place and went on upto the late Canozoic period and even in the Mioscene period. Thus the Koubru hill was formed by about forty million years ago in the Eocene era as proved by the fossils (Kattal) available there.

It is most the probable theory that the chain of hills which encircle the valley and the knolls inside, might have been developed under such processes as mentioned above and it seems that the hills of Manipur grew up set by set leaving the great silted lake in the centre ,which later on formed the valley. Thus the valley itself was under the water for many years. In course of time, the water was drained and erosion from the surrounding hills led to the formation of a beautiful valley in the centre. The latest report of the geological survey of the Deccan proved that the valley was under the water some"2000 years ago (B.P.).

Habitation in this country started from the hills as the valley was under water. No doubt there were some people living in the marshy land also. By the beginning of the Christian era or a little earlier the ancestors of the nine salais started descending in the valley and altogether left the hills. Thus the hills became home of the local tribes. There are references in the Manipuri chronicles that some tribes too followed their masters and were living at different places in the valley.[4] But sooner or later they left the valley and returned to the hills. Their examples were followed by some Salai members. So we find many groups of Meiteis of different clans in the hills even in the late Christian era.

Geographical position of Manipur is such that it is cut off from the Indian mainstream and the west. On the other hand the hills of Manipur were the best place for hiding of different refugees coming from east and west. Political pressure and other minor causes led to migration of different ethnic groups over this country at the beginning of her history who became overlord of local tribes in due course. They cultivated matrimonial alliance with the local tribes and their off shoots became ancestors of the present Meiteis. So, there is an unbroken tie between the two groups viz, the Meiteis and local tribes. Biological appearance between the two communities is the best proof of it.

History of the Meitei started from the arrival of two refugees viz. Atingkok and Amamba Shidaba alias Hung who migrated to this place escaping from a terrible war. They were warmly received by one Taibangpanbagi-mapu, who was the then ruler of Thingrum hill, later Koubru hill. From Koubru hill they shifted immediately to Kurum hill alias Chingkhei Nonghum Shang. From there Atingkok started political organization under the advice of the Taibangpanbagimapu.[5] It opened a new chapter. Thus Atingkok was regarded as founder chief or generalized ancestor of the Meiteis. After the retirement of the Taibangpanbagimapu, Atingkok took the title of the former.

During the period the country was inhabited by ten important tribes in four directions . The people of the east (East Manipur) was known as Trang-trang or Trang or trang-trangpai. Their face was round shaped. The next group who were inhabitants of the north, having partly round shaped face were known as Haorei. The westerners were called Ashang-apum or Ashangbam-Arambam. Their facial structure was similar to that of the horse. The last group was called Pongkhu-ponghan. The group consisted of seven different tribes. They had pointed face.[6] Thus at the beginning of their history, the country was inhabited by ten different ethnic groups regardless of the local tribes. Local tribes were huge in number, having more than fifty different groups.

Meanwhile another great power arrived at chingkheinonghum ching. He was none but the Atiya-Kuru Shidaba. Atiya moved from the south (Kale division of Kabaw valley) and halting at different places arrived at Kurum hill. He was able to subdue Hung and forcibly took the seat of the latter i.e. Loiren Khunbirok at Kurum hill.[7] Later on he was able to bring Atingkok under his control. Accordingly Atingkok recognised him as a son and handed over the charge of undertaking the political organization i.e. the task of subduing the local tribes. It is termed as 'Leishemba' in the Meitei Chronicles. Atingkok then retired at Loiren Phirenyai at Mongpa Chigmahut (Pishum hillock).[8] Accordingly Atingkok advised Asiba alias Sanamahi who arrived recently at Chingkhei nonghum shang to assist Atiya. It was accepted, the joint effort of Atiya and Asiba (Konsouren) was able to conquer four principalities on the hills (Nonglon) and four in the valley (Leikha) i.e. on the slope of hills and mounts. By the moment there arose a misunderstanding or clash between Atiya and Asiba. So, Atiya handed over the whole task to Asiba.[9] Sooner or later Asiba was able to complete the work of creating Leirol mapal and Nonglol mapal i.e. nine principalities on the hills and nine principalities on the slopes of the hills or mounts as directed by Atingkok. Then he made arrangement for settlement of his newly founded principalities by inviting outsiders and provided them necessities of life.

It was due to his contribution, Sanamahi was regarded as a generalized ancestor i.e. Poklen-Pokpa-Satlen Shatpa.

He was then exalted to the position of supreme deity. (Lai Kasha)

Meanwhile with the effort of Atiya Kuru Shidaba, Ching ahum-len-Ahum, invited Konjin-tingthokpa alias Apanba from Keng-Kang (Chaingkhoang). Present Xiangkhoang in Lao.[10]

He usurped the power of Sanamahi and became overlord of the country. Sanamahi then retired to Koubru hill.[11] Then there ensued a long struggle for power between the two. But the attempt of Sanamahi was fruitless. In spite of all this there was no peace and tranquility in the state. Accordingly Atiya advised Apanba to make a compromise with Sanamahi which was executed. Accession of Konjin tingthokpa marked a turning point in the history of the Meitei. Thus the dream of Atingkok became real.

The period from the arrival of AtingkoJk to the accession of Konjintingthokpa is described in the Manipuri chronicles as a period of creation (Leishemba). But political expansion and its consolidation continued. As in the case of Indian mythology, Manipuri also followed the system of having four eras viz. Hayi chak, Haya chak, Langba (Khunnung-Langba) chak and Kona chak. The system was prototype of the Indian era having local names. But it is doubted that the period of the eras varies from that of the Indian system. The period of creation (Leishemlon) took place in the first era i.e. Hayi chak and settlement started from the second era. But proper history of civilization started from the third era i.e. Langba chak. After Konjintingthokpa the country was ruled by different salais. The total number of kings, who ruled over this country from the beginning of Hayi chak upto the beginning of Kona chak (before Nongda lairen) was 111 altogether 84 (eighty four) coronated kings and 27 twenty seven uncoronated kings belonging to all salais.[12]

But some local scholars mistakably considered that the said kings were ruling in succession after Apanba. So they tried to place the beginning of the Meitei history some 3000-2000 years before the accession of Nongdalairen or 3000-2000 B.C. which cannot be acceptable. It is clearly stated in their chronicles that the eighty four was the total number of kings who ruled at different places during the four eras. (Ningthou-mariphumari-teina-teinapalamye).[13] Even though their theory is unacceptable still there is the problem of chronology not only for the B.C. but also for the early parts of the Christian era, right from the accession of nongda Lairen (33 A.D.) to Naothingkhong (8th century A.D.).

Again the date of the arrival of Atingkk is also in mystery. It is probable that the event took place from 4th to 3rd century B.C. from the following facts.

1. The great war which led to the migration of Atingkok and Luwang tribe might be Chinese attack of Yunan in the 3rd century B.C. during the Hsan period. Their attacks led to the migration of many aboriginal tribes of Yunan and Kochin China in different directions. Thus , the Mru or Lawang tribe reached Manipur and one section went as far as Arakan.(l)
2. Since the genealogical trees of all the clans (salais) contain eleven generations in average right from the beginning up to the accession of Nongda lairen (from 1st century A.D.), the event of Atingkok took place some three or four generations earlier i.e. third to fourth century B.C.

3. Eastern expansion of Kalinga took place by about 3rd century B.C. A list of kings having the suffix of Raja viz. Chekaraja, Amuraja, Khakaraja etc. is found in the Nganba Khumuchamlol from the fourth generation of the salai.[14] It is a fact that some Kalinga princes were ruling over in Manipur from the 3rd century B.C. If the list of the kings * that is found in the Nganba Khumuchamlol were Kalinga princes, the history of the Meitei started from 3rd century B.C. or a little ahead i.e. from the 4th century B.C.

The above facts proved that the event of Atingkok's arrival or beginning of the history of Meitei started from 4th to 3rd century B.C. But it will be safe to make the final judgement after making a proper assessment of the Manipuri eras and making a comparative study of the Indian system.

Proto History of Manipur

History of the Meitei is divided into four eras from the beginning of creation upto present day. They were Hayi chak, Haya chak, Langba chak and Kona chak. Accession of Nongda lairen took place at the beginning of the last era i.e. Kona chak. During the first three eras, eighty four kings were ruling this country. Number of kings who ruled at different eras was as follows.

1.	Hayi chak	- 21
2.	Haya chak	- 26
3.	Langba chak	- 37
	Total	- 84

(excluding uncornated kings) (133)

After Konjintingthokpa another salai became the overlord of the country. The new salai was known as Nganba. The first king of this Salai was one Poireileishangthou-hanba-khunung nganba mapu alias Nganba Khaiphaba thonga temphaba. Some scholars identified him as Konjintingthokpa. He made his capital at Koksang (Chingkhei hill).[15] He is identified as the head of the nine Laibungthou. It seems that he moved from the south and became the head or overlord of the nine Laibubgthou. The period of the nine Laibungthou was a landmark in the history of the land.

Territorial jurisdication of Manipur was extended in different directions.References are found in their chronicles that Thangjing was the master of Tripura (Takhel-lakchin phamba), Cachar (Mayang-sakan-tongba) and Bengal (Pangan Tampak-Koiba).[16] Similarly other Laibugthous too could achieve much success. So, from a very early period contact was made with the west and the Manipuris had connection with North east Indian states.

After Poireileishangthou hanba one Kangba was the ruler of the country making his capital at Mongpi hill (Chingmeirong). It is said that he was the son of the mythical Konjin tingthokpa. The sons of Kangba were ruling at different places of the country but some migrated in the neighbouring countries. The rule of the Sarangleishangthem clan marked the beginning of a new era called Haya chak . The first king of this salai was one 'Srang'. His capital was at Thanghutwa (langol hill). His son Leishang succeeded him.[17]

But sooner or later one Tari took the overlordship of the country. He made his capital at Khupunching (Selei-Langmai ching).[18]

After Tari the Ke-Ke Salai once more took the power. Their capital was at Thanghutwa, from there they shifted to Moirang and settled there permanently and became a section of Moirang clan. Ke-Ke Salai was succeded by the Luwang clan. They were the last dynasty of the era.[19]

The rule of Angom clan marked the beginning of another era known as Langba-chak. They made their capital at Kongba Maru (Pukhao).[20]

Angom clan was replaced by Nongyai alias Khuman. Their capital was at Laipong.[21] After the fall of Nongyai, one Mariya Phambalcha (Nganba-Khumukcham) became overlord of the country. He founded the system of counting years.[22] His regin took place some 5089 years (B.P) in the Meitei year.

Mariya was followed by king Kakshuba of Mangang clan. His capital was at Koubru hill.[23] The long reign of Manang clan was brought to an end by a great war which has been recorded as natural calamity in the Meitei chronicles. It was probably the attack of the Nanchou (Ngailao). According to Panthoibi Khongul, the event took place during the reign of one Sapaiba a suitor to Panthoibi. But Khaba dynasty under one Khaba Leirenhan is described as the master of the land. He continued to rule upto the accession of Nongda lairen Pakhangba. According to Singkak there was the rule of Pong for five years before Nongda.[24]

So it is probable that the calamity as mentioned in the Meitei chronicle might be the attack of the Pong (Nagalilao) who ruled the country through their agent i.e. khaba Leirenhan.

Accession of Nongda Lairen was a turning point in the history of Manipur. His accession marked the beginning of a new era i.e.Kona chak. The king was regarded as the incarnation of the mythological Konjintingthokpa. So scholars focus all their attention, making him the generalized ancestor, spiritual and cultural head.

While writing the history of Manipur it was a fashion among the local scholars to give the history of the Ningthouja clan only. But in reality it was a wrong process. The chiefs of the different clans and local tribes were also ruling over this country along with the Ningthouja clan. But it is fact that Ningthouja clan subdued and annexed the principalities of the neighbouring chiefs one after another which ultimately formed the Meitei state in the 15th century A.D. So early history of Manipur was the history of the inter clan fight for supremacy. At the end the luck favoured the Ningthouja clan.

A list of the sixty seven kings and few nameless kings from outside was there on the throne of Ningthouja clan from 1st century A.D. to!891 A.D. i.e. from Nongda lairen to Kulaehandra. Out of the 67 kings the names of Naophangba, Nongthingkhong, Khongtekcha, Irengba, Loyumba, Thawanthaba, Khumbomba, Ningthoukhomba, Kyamba, Mungyanba, Khagemba, Charairongba, Garibaniwaj, Bhagyachandra, Chourajit, Marjit, Gambhir Singh, Nara singh, Surchandra, Kulachandra etc. are worth mentioning.

From amongst the nine clans, Khaba, Nganba, Chenglei, Haorok Konthou and Luwang lost their power in the early part of the Christian era. But a section of the Luwang clan i.e. Heirem-Khunjan ran to the south and occupied Lamangdong and its neighbouring area giving constant trouble to the Khuman clan. According to the request of the Khuman king (Adon Punshiba) the combined force of Ningthouja and Khuman defeated and subdued them for ever in the 13th century A.D.(l) After that they made some fruitless attempt to revolt against the khuman clan. The section of Luwang i.e. Lang-maibarol, came down from the Langmai hill under the leadership of Nungkhongba, Ayangjambaleikhamphaba and Haobatekpa and settled at Khurai as the peaceful subjects of the Ningthouja clan.[25]

Khaba clan declined forever after their fight with the Ningthouja clan during the reign of Nongda lairen. During the reign of Naokhamba effort was made to exterminate the clan completely. Accordingly they merged into different clans viz. Angom, Khuman and Nganba.[26] Thus a new salai known as Kha-Nganba was formed. But nothing is known about their future activities.

Angom clan was subdued during the time of Shameirang (6th century A.D.). Their king was directed to come down from Langmai hill by King Urakonthouba (8th century A.D.) and finally allotted the village of present Angom leikai as his seat.[27] During the reign of Chalamba (16th century A.D.) the clan could recover their lost power and was able to reassert independence. They overthrew the power of the Ningthouja king (Chalamba). But their reign was short lived, they put one Mungyamba (1562-1597) On the throne of Ningthouja clan and became peaceful subject of the Ningthouja kings.[28] Once again, during the reign of king Charairongba, (17th century A.D.) they became powerful but were subdued forever.

History of Sarang- Leishangthem clan during the Christian era is in obscurity. Accession of Nongda Lairen marked the beginning of their downfall. They moved towards the east and settled on the foot of the Nongmaijing hill at Taknakha. But being pressed by the Angom clan, they went to the south and settled at Leishanghiden(Leishangthem)

They merged with the Chenglei salai and exist till now as a separate clan. One Chingjennaranpanganba of the clan challenged the authority of the king Naophangba of the Ningthouja clan (5th to 6th century A.d.) but was defeated after a long fight. Even though his brother Taopung Khongtonpa some how restored their ancestral throne, the clan gradually lost its importance and declined for ever.

Of the two powers of the south Khuman was one of them. In the early days they were very powerful and were able to keep their independence upto 14th century A.D. making matrimonial alliance with the Ningthouja clan. But frequent drought in their principiality and other supersticious reasons finally led to the submission of their king (Lamyai-Kaikhinba) to Kongyanba (1323-1335), the king of Ningthouja. Lamyaikaikhinba along with his followers arrived at Kanglei and settled in the present seat of Purana Rajbari, from there they moved to Wangkhei leikai.[29]

Annexation of Moirang in the 15th century A.D. brought the unification of the state. Punshi Khurenchanba the thirty sixth king of the clan was murdered by a conspiracy organized by the king Ningthoukhomba of the Ningthiuja clan. In retaliation the people of Moirang invaded the principality of Ningthouja clan. But there also by the conspiracy of their minister (Chaoba) they were completely routed out.[30] The defeat brought about their decline for ever. Thus Moirang became a part of Meitei state as Tampak loi.[31]

Thus the early history of Manipur upto 15th century A.D. is the history of internal fight amongst the clans.The clash for supremacy was common feature of those days, which ultimately led to the gradual downfall of all other clans except the Ningthouja. Thus under the aegis of the Ningthouja clan an unified state was formed in the 15th century A.D. Besides the internal fight amongst themselves, they met foreign invasion from the neighbouring countries viz. Shan state (Pong), Burmese(Awa), Kabo, Tripura (Takhel),Cachar (Mayang) and Ahom (Tekhao). Thus Manipur was under the subjugation of the Shan and Burmese at intervals. But it was short lived.Sooner or later Meitei kings reasserted their independence. Even though there was an endless clash for supremacy amongst the clans, in the case of danger and foreign invasion they fought together .for a common cause. By way of example, king Khumbomba (1263-1278) helped the Khumans in their fight against the invasion of Kabo and was able to repulse them successfully.[32]

Even though foreign invasion were short lived, the consequences were far reaching. They left some permanent cultural impacts on the Meitei society. The invasions of Calofen, Samlung and others in the 8th and 14th century A.D. respectively brought about a cultural revolution in the state. Not only Buddhism was introduced in the state, but also the Meiteis' way of life was considerably improved, probably Shan culture was introduced here. Burmese occupation of the state could exert similar influence. Similarly western culture began to penentrate through foreign invasion.

By way of example, Cachari invasion of 1606 A.D. brought the Muslims of East Bengal in Manipur. It was a landmark in her (Meitei) cultural evolution. Muslim way of life, style, art and craft and costume was introduced in the state during the reign of King Khagemba. Besides the political pressure, religious peachers from the east and west brought the oriental and western cultures throughout the ages.

Again inclusion of foreigners i.e. Nongpok haram and early migration was peaceful but their cultural outburst was loud sounding and had far reaching effect. So there was continuous cultural expansion in the state from the east and west, bringing about a synthesis which ultimately led to mould up a distinct culture of her (Meitei) own.

In cultural belt Manipur was more akin to the south east Asia. The characteristic feature of the south east Asian culture was Hindu culture mixed up with the indigenous culture of the local tribes. At the same time, Manipur was an important passage from India via south east Asia to China in the early days. Heirok range was one of such passes. So there have been frequent cultural contact and interaction of the two mainlands i.e the east and west. Besides, political adventurers and refugees from different directions specially from the east arrived in Manipur and settled here permanently. They cultivated matrimonial alliance with local tribes and other inhabitants and started a new history here. Their offshoots became the ancestors of the present Meitei peoples. Thus we find elements of two divergent cultures.

Some of the striking features of the Maru (Lawang) cultures that were adopted by the Meiteis are premarital sexual relations, courtship of adolescent boys in the front apartment of the house in the evening, taking of huge bride price, giving of dowry on limited scale, taboo for marriage among the same clan, preference for cross cousin marriage, to look after the parents by the youngest son,ancestor worship, Shamanism and divination.Similarly, the Meo or Miao (Hung or Lai-salai) could exert influence in the Meitei society in many aspects viz. performance of elaborate rite and rituals to ward off the evil spirits, to appease the local or guardian gods, agricultural ceremony, rain calling ceremony, animal sacrifices, and practice of primary and secondary burial. They have the trace of such culture till now.

Similarly,mythical god Konchintingthokpa commonly known as Pakhangba was invited from XiangKhoang in Lao. Their chronicles described the event as "Ching ahum-len ahumna-pakhangbabu Senkang or Kenkang dagi Kouruiye" He (Pakhangba) most probably belonged to Kha-Ko or KhaKou or Akha a section of Mon Annam peoples. Elop ement, the most preferable mode of marriage in the Meitei society was probably brought from northern Lao. Other points of similarity are hair style, laws of divorce, laws of inheritance, ancestors worship, veneration of three deceased ancestor,(Phungga-apokpa).The above facts clearly infer that, some elements of southeast Asian culture specially of Indo China were brought here by the immigrants.

Above all, their mythical god Sanamahi is also an outsider. At the same time chronicles like Laihou naophamlon mentioned about the settlement of Shan (Pong) peoples at the beginning of her history (hayichak). Sanamahi is described as generalized and supreme ancestor (Poklen pokpa satlen satpa).Nowadays revivalist groups of Meiteis venerate Sanamahi as supreme deity. Naturally, Shan culture began to infiltrate in the Meitei culture. On account of its kin similarity some scholars pointed out that, Meitei culture is prototype of Shan culture.

Again the Lisu or Leisu tribe who is regarded as ancestors of the Sarangleishang or Chenglei brought the elements of Tibetan culture. The tribe lived together with Tibetans for about three generations before they moved towards north east India. In a similar way influence of Boro

Cachari is there in many aspects of the Meitei culture. The system of disposal of the dead, mode of cremation in particular may be regarded the very system of the Cacharis. The north western hills of Manipur including koubru hill was once under their domination. Koubru hill is described as Thongnang melei ching (hill of thongnang people) before the coming of the present name.

We have discussed earlier that there was wave of migration in the land and these tribes were able to subdue the local tribes and became the master of the land. They became ancestors of the present Meiteis. Besides the political changes they also brought a cultural revolution in due course. Some prominent political leaders viz. Atingkok maru sidaba, Hung, Konjintinthokpa, Sanamahi, Poireiton etc. added fragments of their cultural traits here and a synthesis of these elements moulded up a new culture of the land which became the present Meitei culture.

Then again, religious missionaries and political adventurers brought Indian culture one after another. The Sakya princess from Kapilabastu (Binnakaraja) brought here a crude from Hinduism(Hinduism of the pre Buddhist and jain periods). A little later a prince of the same clan (Dhajaraja, 6th century B.C.) brought Buddhism in course of his asylum in Kabaw valley (Burma). After that Kalinga (Maithilee) introduced Hinduism (Sakta or Shaivism) in course of their political expansion in the east.

Indian culture was extended here not only from the west but also from the east too. As for instance, a Buddhist missionary from Burma arrived in the court of king Maputhiba of the Angom clan. During the Christian era Shan adventurers like Co- lofen, Samlungpha and others induced the Meiteis to accept Buddhism and to modify their way of life during their political subjugation of the state. Thus wave after wave and generation after generation, Indian culture began to influence Meitei culture which ultimately led to mould up a new culture of her own, peculiar to the south east Asian culture. It was the synthesis of the east, west and indigenous culture.

According to Ptolemy Manipur was under Brahmanical rule during the period of Kalinga expansion. Even after the fall of Brahmanical rule here, Brahmanism was there without any]jreists or experts to conduct religious sacrifices and others. It was conducted by the local preists (i.e. maiba and maibi) in their own fashion.[33]

Western expansion did not stop altogether, sooner or later many enthusiastic preachers crossed the western ranges and attempts were made to convert the Manipuries to their respective faiths. Among them the events of king Naophangba and Irengba may be mentioned. Frequent attacks by Burmese and Shan brought a halt to the Aryan culture specially in the process of Sanskritisation. Due to this constant non-Aryan invasion the Aryan culture in Manipur became nearly lifeless.[34] Thus Hinduism became a new form in Manipur in the 18th century A.D.

Like the current of a river takes different manifestations at each and every bend of the river, the Meitei culture also underwent changes from time to time. With the advent of the Christian era, the Meitei culture has been constantly changing its feature throughout the ages. Since the Meitei Puyas (Chronicles) which depict certain periods in question had been written mostly in the 17th and 18th centuries, it is difficult to accept as true all the accounts described in those puyas. The Meitei culture as was extant upto 16th century was the composite culture formed by the continuous current of history with different cultural fragments of different epochs. As such the image of an essential culture began to manifest only in the 17th century after the different features of culture in the previous epochs had merged into a composite cultures. However, it can be assumed that the culture that was extant before the 17th century was a form of south east Asian culture with the mixture of Indian culture.

REFERENCES

1 Kummel. History of Earth pp. 2-3.

2. G. Gyaneswar :- Geomophelogical analysis of Manipur. Paper published in all India congress-1977. Calcutta.

3. Kummel opcit, p. 3.

4. Langdai Langhei. (Unpublished chronicle) pp. 11-12

5. Y. Bhagya Leithak leikharon p. 9 also see Pudin.

6. I. Amubi - Leihou Naophamlon. p. 6.

7. Khununglon. (U.ch) p. 12.

8. Thirel nanamba-(U.ch) p. 6.

9. Y. Bhagya-opcit, p. 29.

10. Mangi- Chakparol P. 1 also see Tangkru lamlen (u.ch)

11. Y. Bhagya opcit- p. 37.

12. Khunnglon Singkak (U.ch) Lathup.

13. Maputhiba (U.ch).

14. Sangai phamang. (relevant part of Kanghujamlon)

15. Langdang Langhei, p.28. also see Leihou naophamlon, p. 7.

16. Sanamahi-laihui (U.ch), p. 20.

17. I. Amubi. Opcit, p. 7 also see langdai langhei.

18. Ibid, p.8.

19. Lai Khunda (U.ch,Lathup).

20. I. Amubi Opcit, p. 8. see Langdai langhei.

21. Laikhunda. (U.ch).

22. I. Amubi. Opcit, p. 8-see Langdai langhei.

23. Khundarol (U.ch. Lathup).

24. Singkak-(U.ch).
25. N. Ibochouba. Thirel meiramliba, p. 19 also see Chingoirol, p. 54..
26. Kh. Yaima. Pakhangba Phambal, p. 46 see also I-tinnaba.
27. Angom Khonghou-(U.ch.lathup).
28. Puwari. (U.ch lathup).
29. N.Khelchandra Khuman kangleiron, pp. 49-50.
30. Miyat (U.ch), pp. 16-19.
31. Kei-loi-lingkhatpa-(U.ch).
32. N. Khelchandra-opcit, pp. 49-50. also see Cheitharol Kumbaba, p. 7.
33 Maputhiba :- (u.ch), pp. 35-36.
34. Girinni :- Researches on Pholemy geography of Eastern Asia, pp. 31-32 also see The history of Bengal by Jadunath Sarkar, p. 227.

CHAPTER ONE

BIRTH AND BIRTH CEREMONY

Concept of Birth

The soul is regarded as an image of the Almighty God. The Almighty God sends over this earth one's soul for a life with a mission with certain obligations. In the beliefs of the Meiteis, the soul before its birth as a human being passed through different natural objects on its passage from the Almighty God to the womb of a mother. So,an issueless person begged the Almighty God for having a child. There are many tales and beliefs, how an issueless person got a child with the blessing of the God. Their chronicles also mention some specific rite and rituals to beget the child. The passages of the soul are as follows:-

1) Almighty God.
2) Numit (Sun).
3) Tha (Moon).
4) Thaba (Evening star).
5) Shajik (Morning star).
6) Okpuroi.
7) Thahuireng.

8) Father, (the father kept with him the soul for two months with him)

9) Mother.

The mother by carrying it for ten months, the child is born. So, the soul passed through six objects stated above from the Almighty God and reached the father, then the father carrying it for two months gave it to the mother in the form of sperm.

The first two months are in a formless stage. On the third month it became the shape of a ball. Then it began to take the form of a human being after the completion of the four months. Next month the child became lively and its head began to lower down and stayed there for a complete one month. It was on the completion often months the child is born.[1] There is also an interesting myth about the baby coming out from the womb of the mother on this earth.

They like a good child, so they followed and observed certain norms of co-habitation. At the same time they carefully study and know how and when a woman conceived. Under their theory so long as the partners are not in full feeling there can't be the conceived. Above all, to get a good or extra-ordinary child they abstain from co-habitation on certain days like, the three days of menstruation, birth days of the husband and wife, full moon and new moon, the days of gods and day time. Late night was most preferable. But hardly, they followed the norms.

To save the blooming child from abortion, they used to perform some rituals during the period of pregnancy on certain specific months. On the third month the evil spirit like Lai amangba was warded off. It was believed that such a spirit caused the abortion and premature death (Poklasira-pola-sira touba). Again, to get a healthy child the mother was invited for a meal by her parents and provided with whatever curry she chooses on the fourth month of the pregnancy. On the ninth month an incantation ceremony of Anam-athou and Konyai hunba (Soul calling ritual) was performed for having a free delivery of the child. It was followed by a process of Anamathou' Kokpiba by the husband in the last month for the same reason if required.[2]

Nature of Delivery

The delivery of the child was usually done in their own house. An expert called Chabokpi maibi and an assistant ie. Mayoknabi conducted the delivery. Just after the baby came out of the mother womb, the umbilical cord was held by the Maibi and shit the cord toward the baby for three times. Then it was cut off by a bamboo knife. For the royal family it was done with an iron knife specially made for the purpose. The baby, after being cleaned and covered with a soft cloth, was handed over to the father. The latter gave the god's name to the child by murmuring the rite to the ear of the child. It was the first ceremony for giving the name of the god (Laiming -Piba). After the ceremony, the baby was handed over to the mother. In the mean time, a women having new child was requested to give milk to the baby. Some scholars are of the opinion that, before Hindunisation the Meities like the Kabui tribe put a few drops of Kalei (Intoxicated liquor) to the mouth of the baby. It was the first occasion of food giving to a newly born baby.

The umbilical cord was kept in an earthen pot along with a coin, seven grains of white rice, seven grains of red rice and was covered by a lid. The pot was buried on the side of the house in different direction according to the gender of the baby. If the baby is a boy it will be on the right side and on the left side for the girl. Due ceremony was performed in its burial. A hole was made having the depth of about one foot and fire was kindled to drive out evil spirit there. Then a coin was offered to the mother earth for permission. But for the royal family the ritual of Konyai hunba (pieces of gold and silver) was used to be performed. By placing the pot which contains the umbilical cord will be covered by earth and pressed softly not to affect the pot. They have the beliefs that, if pressed hard, the child might be deaf and if the hole is very shallow it may cause vomiting tendency to the baby (Khoidou thenba). Meities took special care for umbilical cord with the beliefs that, it served the way to heaven after death. The spirit visited the place where it was buried. So the place was considered as one of the abode of the spirit (god). After the end of all works the members present were provided with food and drinks as a sort of enjoyment and for the blessing of the newly born baby. For the royal family it was performed on a large scale with some entertainment and the ritual of Kasha paotakpa was also held as information to the god Kasha who was also regarded as the master (incharge) of the birth and death.

Care for the mother

Due care was taken for the mother for a period of five days. It was already stated that, the delivery took place in their own house. The place of delivery was chosen either in the first room or last room of the house. But generally they took the last room of the typical Meitei house. In the last room a new bed generally made of straw was stretched near the hearth. There the mother stay for a period of five days. She was provided with only the boiled rice with dry fish and roasted salt. The periods of the five days was known as Maning Kumba. On the sixth day both the mother and child took their bath and cut off nails. The bed used by them was removed and a new bed was either prepared or took her former bed. From that day simple food with simple curry was taken for full one month.

Ipan Thaba(birth ritual)

The ritual for birth was known as Ipan thaba. After Hindunisation the name was changed to Swasti pujah and Hindu ritual was also added. The ritual of Ipan thaba was divided into two parts. The first part was performed in the morning and the second part on the night of the same day. In the early days, the ritual was held on the 5/6th day of the birth of the child according to the gender of the baby. If the baby was a male it was held on the 6th day and on the 5th day for female. But later on under the influence of Hinduism the ritual began to be performed on the 6th day regardless of gender. Some scholars gave their views that the name Ipan thaba owed its origin from the word Yupanthaba i.e. giving of Yu (intoxicated liquor) to the baby as stated above.

Ritual in the morning

The ritual for birth was known as Ipan thaba. The first part of the ritual was held in the morning of the 5/6th day of the birth of the baby. The main theme of the ritual was to propitiate the goddess of Ipan leima alias Pithraibi Khongdaibi. The second item of the ritual was to perform a pretended ceremony of food giving (Chaumba) to the child. Before that the rite of Thawaimi Konshinba(soul calling) will be held. The ritual was concluded by the ceremony of handing over of the child to the mother. In the ritual the child will be put on a winnowing fan (Yangkok) and to ward off evil spirits are brunt some local leaves.(Khoiju leikham). The maibi will ask the mother in a poetic form "Do you like your child or gold, silver, coin, winnowing fan etc etc. The grandmother will reply "Nay we like nothing but the child. The Maibi than handed over the child to the grandmother and in turn she gave the baby to the mother. For the royal family the ritual of Kasha Paotakpa was also performed.[5]

Night ritual

The birth ritual continued in the night of the same day. It was believed that, the Nongdamba-Lai the God of destination came on the night of the Ipan and writes on the forehead the future destiny of the child. So, a grand ritual to propitiate the god was held for his blessings, and other gods and goddesses like Lainingthou Sanamahi, Leimarel (household deities) Kacheng Nongthangleima. etc were also worshipped.

But it seems that they were later inclusions from the fact that, worship of Lainingthou Sanamahi as household god was introduced only in the 17th century AD during the time of king Khagemba. Prior to that, the Meiteis used to worship Lord Pakhangba. Formality for the worship of the above gods and goddesses over, the expert (Purohit) will make the incantation of bow and arrows which was made specially for the purpose and begged four expert archers of the past viz Khoiri-lintang shitpa, Phunal telheiba, Mende ningthou Haotak laiha and Chairel ninghou to protect the child from evil spirits. An uncle of the baby will shoot one arrow in each direction starting from the north-east ,the last arrow i.e the fifth one was not shoot but simply aimed at to the sky and below and kept inside the house until the baby was grown up in three years.

While the shooting was going on outside, inside the house, the baby was kept over a cloth and the rites of Thawaimi-Konshinba and incantation rite of Irulaishol would be made. Then a robe made of black thread be tied in the hand of the baby with a protective rite.[6]

Now a days a new item known as Dan-thadaba/ Taret-seija Kubiba is added just after the end of the above rituals. The night ritual was concluded by providing food and drinks to all the members present and their blessings to the newly born baby were sought.

Rituals of birth and Hindu influences

Comming of Hinduism has brought about great changes in the rituals of birth ceremony. Garibaniwaj Maharaj (18th century AD) unable to uproot the traditional customs and beliefs made a compromise with the local priests. It was agreed upon that, the morning ritual be retained in tact, but the night ritual be substituted for Hindu rituals and rites. Above it an item of reciting the story of Swasti devi be held in the courtyard of the house accompanied by a Kritan. But some scholars are of the opinion that, the item was later inclusion from the time of Bhagyachandra. So, the present birth rituals of the Meiteis is a synthesis of the traditional practices aAd Hindu custom. But nowadays hardly we find experts in the heart of the Imphal city who can perform the rituals of Ipanthaba i.e. the traditional practices. So, generally morning items began to be dropped gradually.

Yum-Shengba

The last ritual of the birth was Yum shengba. It was believed that, the house has been unclean with the birth of the child. The Meiteis have the same observation in the case of death also. It was known as Yum mangba. During the period of Yum mangba the family and their lineages(Sagei) were under seclusion and did not participate in any religious works. On the 10th day of the birth of the baby the house was clean, old cooking pots were replaced by new ones and performed the incantation ceremony. The mother and the baby were also cleaned and baby was brought outside and prayed the sun god. Medication of the mother (I-Khombiba) was made. For the royal family the ritual of Atai-Iratpa and Kasha- paotakpa were also held. On that day the king rewarded those who were involved directly in the birth of the child. For the management of the functions and rituals the king collected a special tax known as Chabok wangol shelhkai from the inhabitants of the four leikais viz khwai,Yaiskul, Khurai and Wangkhei. (For Meitei kings). The queens too were forced to subscribe certain specific amount of money.[7]

Naming of the child(Angang-maming-thonba)

The other minor item of the life circle ceremony of Meiteis was the naming of the child. There was no hard and first rule for fixing the date of naming. But there was a belief that, if the naming be performed immediately after Ipanthaba,the child will have long life i.e. will not die before the maturity of the life span. There was also no specific rite and ritual for it, the name was just declared by the parents. At the sametime there were no hard and fast rules for giving the name.

Regarding the nature of naming, In one case the name was preceded by the clan name, to cite :-Nungpal Pombiluwaoba (Pombiluwaoba of Nungpal clan), in another case the person was identified by his place of residence. But after Hindunisation, the Meiteis began to use three names i.e. the first indicates the Yumnak (surname). The middle will be the person's name which is followed by Singh like the Punjabis.

Chaumba(first food giving ceremony)

The first food giving to a newly born child was just on the day of the birth of the baby by putting a few drops of alcohol to the mouth of the baby. For about three days the baby was provided with the milk of an adopted mother(Khominbi). Then on the occasion of Ipanthaba there was also a pretended ritual of Chaumba. So the present ritual will be the third occassion of food giving to a newly born child. Generally a baby became acquitant to take solid form of food after a few months. So, the ritual of Chaumba used to be performed when the baby became three months old. But as the boys were not taking much interest in solid food for a longer period so, for them it was usually held in the 5th month. But generally the ceremony was held on the 3rd month for the female child and the 5th month for the male baby.

Almost all the functions of the Meiteis were ceremonious and accompanied by some religious rites and rituals. At the same time omen seeking was a common feature as they were good shamanists and superstitious.

The main theme of the ritual was giving of food to the child which was followed by an omen seeking. The articles for the meal were offered to deities first and then it was prepared for meal. In the early days fish or meat formed the main item of curry and five kinds of paddy formed the meal. But after Hindunisation it was substituted with vegetarian food or Kheer.

In the porch of the house the Almighty god will be propitiated by offering flower, fruits etc and articles for omen seeking like, gold, silver, coin, earth, paddy, book etc and the meal will be displayed. Inside the house, the goddess of wealth and prosperity will be propitiated to give abundant foods throughout the whole life of the child. After the worship was over the child adorned with new attire will be seated over the mother. An expert or father himself by reciting due rites of the Chaumlol will offer the meal five times accompanied by water each time to the baby. The rite must synchronize with the offering of the meal. For royal family it was done by some specific person. The child will be on the arms of the maternal grandmother and the food giver must be from the family of the Shadokpam sagei. Those who were envoived in the ritual were properly rewarded. Expenditure for it was borne by the fees collected from the three queens.[9]

After the food giving ritual was over the process of omen seeking was performed. Articles for omen seeking were displayed before the child as stated above and the child was allowed to touch or hold it. From the article the baby touches first, they predict what the baby likes and which profession the child will be familiar to. As for instances, if the baby touches paddy he/she might be an agriculturalist and have plenty of food in his/her life. The ritual was concluded by a meal or refreshment to the members present.

Na hutpa (Ear boring ceremony)

Like the Hindus the Meiteis also performed the practices and ritual of ear boring. Ear boring ceremony was known as Na-hutpa. (Na = ear, Hutpa = boring) There, is a controversial point of views about the origin of the ritual. Some are of the opinion that, ear boring custom among Meiteis was the influence of Hinduism. On the other hand some scholars strongly refute the point. The custom was prevalent in the country from time immemorial and it was practised by different tribes of Manipur who were never touched by the influence of Hinduism.

Generally ear boring took place in the 3rd year of the child. But references are found for its observation in the 7th year. The nature of ritual was very simple. By performing the due norms of a worship (Iratlol) the Almighty God was informed for ear boring of the child and boring was made with a pointed stick made of bamboo and through the hole was inserted a cotton thread.. The purpose of the ceremony was mainly for the longevity of the child and to protect him from the attacks of the evil spirits. If the child died before ear boring, the reverse system of the disposal of the dead used to be performed and the proper norms of death rituals were forbidden. So, ear boring was an unavoidable and compulsory custom among Meiteis.

Lugun thangba(Investment of sacred threads)

Investment of sacred threads which the Meiteis called Lugun thangba is purely of Hindu Practice. But some Manipuri chronicles mention that the Meiteis adopted the practice from a very early period before the introduction of Hinduism as state religion in the 18th century AD. If the theory is acceptable it is most probable that, a section of Meiteis got Hindu influences from the early periods and adopted the Hindu practice and customs. We find the same confusion in the rituals of the disposal of the dead.In those days only the Piba (head of the Sagei) was allowed to invest the threads (lugun).[11] But the number of strands of thread differs from one group to another (Clan). The number of strands ware - 9-7-5-3. In the beginning of the 18th century the threads was tied to the hair knot instead of keeping it over the shoulder.[12] How far is it true is a matter of further investigation as the authencity of those chronicles is questionable.

Beginning of Education (Shilnaipham Kaba)

The Meiteis gave their children proper training during the period of adolescence. 16 yrs. and 13 yrs. were considered as the age of puberty. With the attainment of the age of puberty they used to send their children for education or proper training of every aspect of life. But like the Naga tribes the system of dormitory was not prevalent. They used to send their children to the house of an expert of their locality in the evening. They went to the house of the male expert and joined the works of the master and learned the works practically, so also the girls in the house of the expert women. The system was known as Shilnaipham Khaba. Thus the girls learnt the arts of spinning, weaving, song, dance, Yumbalol etc, Similarly, the boys got the training of different arts including the art of warfare.

The beginning of learning was considered as an important moment of life in their community. They pay proper tribute to the teachers. Though we can't get any specific rite and rituals for the purpose, it was just like the Vidya rambha ceremony of the Hindu. The Kabui tribe of Manipur performs a nominal ceremony till now.

REFERENCES

1. N. Manijao. Pombi lang, p. 3.
2. W. Tolchousans-Meitei Lairik Mathang p. 4-8
3. O. Bhogeswar-loina Shillol, p. 33.
4. Madhop & Khelchandra ; Khunung leichat shajat. p. 67.
5. Y. Budhichandra Tharol Nongkhairol, p. 52.
6. Ipantha -unpublished Puya.
7. Kh.Chandrashekher- Loiyunba Shilyen, p. 56.
8. Chaumba-Unpublished Puya.
9. Kh. Chandrasekhar-opcit, p. 59-60.
10. Ch. Joy Malem Leishemlol-Ariba, p. 153.
11. Kh. Chandrasekhar- Opcit, p. 8.
12. L. Mangi & L. Mni Singh:- Meitei Puran (Garibaniwaj Charitra), p. 17.

CHAPTER TWO

MARRIAGE AND MARRIAGE CEREMONY

Introduction

The parents allowed the children to choose their mate, but invited the groom's family for the arrangement of the marriage. But there was also the system of go between or engagement. But the general features of the marriage is elopement, (gandharava bibaha of the Hindus). The boy and girl who are in love decide to become husband and wife, the latter leave her parent's house with the boy for the house of the maternal uncle or nearest family and requests for the marriage.Accordingly the parents if accepted make the arrangement for the marriage.

The boy and the girls had the chance of meeting each other at state festival, laiharaoba, games like Likon, Baruni kaba etc. Again the meeting in the porch of the girl in the evening (Koirakpa) was also in vogue. The custom permitted the visit of the adolescent boys to the residence of the girl and allowed them to sit in the porch (mangol) of the house. The girl provided them with fruits, smoke etc. and had the chance to talk and love making started. Thus the girls had also the chance to choose her mate. Similar culture was also there among the tribes of Maru,Kachin and Meo.

There was some sort of pre-martial sexual freedom in the Meitei society of early Christian era, like the Kachins. The tales of Khongchomnubi nongkharol, Mainupemcha etc clearly reveal the custom. Premarital sexual freedom was prevelant in almost every tribal society of south east Asia. But the degree of relation differs from place to place. Again the birth of child by unmarried girls was also very common in those days. But in Manipur, if the parent ever detected the case, the daughter was turned out from the family. They have little chance of marriage.

Another interesting aspect of the then society was the freedom of the married women and their free sexual relation with other person. Almost all the important figure of the early Meitei society which are now being worshipped as their deities had more than one husband. To cite few examples, Laikhurembi was the legal wife of Thongarel, but she was handed over to Nongda lairen Pakhangba by changing her name as Laishna. This woman had ellicit connection with Khaba Panthongba and born Khuiyoitompok. So, she had three husbands viz, Thongarel, Nongda Lairen and Khaba Phantongba.Similarly, Laihaotabi had three husband viz Thawarel/Thongarel,Poireiton and Nongbal Pombi Luwaoba. So, there was the element of polyandry in some section of the Meitei society. Again, it was also a common feature to take forcibly the wife of the vanquished rulers by the conquerors in the war. In spite of all these, Meitei kings tried at their best level, to protect the rights and previledges of the women's and immoral traffic by establishing a women court by name " Pacha-Loishang" presided over by chief queen right from the time of Nongda lairen pakhangba(lst century AD).

Monogamy was common feature, but the system of Polygamy was there among the rich and aristrocrate family.

At the same time, there was also the system of Polyandry during the pre-Christian and early part of Christian era in some section of their society. Some scholars pointed out that,, a matrilineal society preceded the present patrilineal one where women were free and absolute like the Khasi of Meghalaya.

The system was probably derived from Tibet. The progenitors of Sarang Leishang clan were once living together with the Utaic race of Tibet where there was women sovereign. (Ethnic history of Shans relevant part of the cradle of the Shan race. AR Colquhaun p.XI). The present marriage system with elaborate rituals having deep philosophical idea owed its origin only from the last quarter of the 18th century AD when they became Hindu. Prior to that, the process of marriage was simple and short and its purpose was only for free sexual union and nothing more. Meitei word for marriage was Nuhongba (Nu = Penis?, Hongba=plenty) free availability or permission for free sex. The present concept of ekka Prana-ekka dehe (one body one soul) was later development after Hindunisation.

There were different process for becoming husband and wife viz marriage by engagement (haina shingnaba), by elopement (chenba). It was common form of marriage in the then Meitei society and at present and thirdly forcible taking of a girl as wife (Nupi chingba) and inducing her to accept either by request or force. There has been a confusion between the second and third one, whatever may be the method, the tie was solemnized by one of the three rituals viz,l) Luhongba,2) Keina Katpa and 3) Loukhatpa, according to their convinences. The system is still in practice. Some scholars are of the opinion that the present system was of late development in the 18thcentury AD as stated above.

The question here is that, what type of ritual was there as a means of solemnizing the tie. It is not an easy question to answer as the Chronicles are quite silent about it. Engagement (go between) for marriage, giving of huge bride price, Heiching Kharai puba, sending of bride from the house of her parent to the groom's house were a few accounts given in their chronicles and tales. But the account for ritual or process of their solemnizing the tie is quite silent.

Marriage system of the Meitei was varied and elaborate. In the early days the system both polyandry and polygamy were there. But with the introduction of patrilineal society the system of polyandry discountinued but polygamy continued to exist. In spite of all these there is still heritage of polyandry in the Meitei society. Again there were different forms of becoming husband and wife i.e. marriage in a loose sense. The system of marriage was very much akin or similar to southern Tais and Black Tais with some local variation.

Polyandary

A system of having or acquiring more than one husband by a woman at a time. The system of polyandry is unknown in the present Meitei society. The present form of society is based on a patrilineal structure which is the heritage of the 17th and 18th century A.D. Before the introduction of the present system there was a heritage of matrilineal form of society, in which polyandry was a form of marriage. As a part of its heritage, there was the case of sexual laxity amongst some Manipuri women. Even today there are cases of having secret husbands which they called Murumba or Mawangangnaba. But the custom does't permit such system, whenever it was to light the women was either shut up in the house or expelled from the house. Tha state

Government also punished them by process of humiliation (Khongoinaba) or forced the man to take the woman and give compensation to the former husband or they were exiled.

Heritage of Polyandry

Manipuri folk tales, traditional saying, even the marriage rules give the account of sexual relation amongst the wives of intimate friends. So,even though it was very common to exchange their children into marriage there was the case of restriction on the ground of possible intermixture of blood. It is said that, under some cases, the woman frankly disclosed the union (sexual union) to her husband and no severe action was taken and the negotiation stopped.

The relation between the housewife and other members of the family specially the brothers of the husband is an attractive point for discussion. A housewife used to address the elder brothers of the husband as Itei and the younger as Inaonupa. A housewife used to keep a piece of cloth or part of the cloth used by her over her head before the matei as a sign of respect and the custom did not permit to make them close and touchability was completely forbidden. Such traditional style was nothing but to prevent sexual relation between the two. But the right to access and the paying court was given to the younger brothers i.e. Manounupa. On the other hand, the wife of the elder brother (Iteima) was looked upon as a person to whom one could openly, though not legitimately, pay court.

Again the restriction imposed upon housewife and Matei was probably enacted to prevent forcible connection or inducement for sexual pleasure by Matei, who is senior member of the family with higher status. As in the case of the younger brothers (B.I.L), the woman (H.W.), by dint of her seniority or status could easily avert any such attempt. From the above norms and its significance, it can be concluded that, there was the system of polyandry in the Meitei society long before the introduction of the present system. The present system replaced the old one, but some of its image is still found in the present social structure. Polyandry was a common form of marriage in almost every matrilineal society. Here in Manipur, the present system (patrilineal) has succeeded a matrilineal society. Besides, the terms like Itei,Inaonupa and matei-manao clearly indicate heritage of polyandry in the Meitei society which has banned with the introduction of present system. The word Matei or Itei, meant a person liable to have union of blood (sexual union) i.e and authorized person for sexual relation, husband in strict sense. The present marriage rule also gives permission to marry a woman of nearest blood or kin, if it is permitted by mingou (Matei thokpa) i.e. terms used to address themselves. Marriage of wife's sister and cross cousin marriage was in vogue in early times, but the system of marrying wife's sister is still continuing.

As among Kotas of Nilgiri, there was intimacy and free acess between the matei and younger susters of the wife (Manao nupi). Their intimacy and permission of the guardian to look after Manaonupi clearly shows heritage of polyandry system. Some of its heritage is still found in the Meitei society.

Again, in the early stage of civilization women were absolutely free in their married life. Tradition says that, some of their ancestors (lairembis) left their husbands without any information or at will and united with another one. Then sooner or later, they returned to their former husbands either by inducement or by some other means. There is a controversy about having common wife or taking brother's wife by younger brother in mythology. Nongthangleima is described as the wife of both Sanamahi and Pakhangba and Leinaothabi was given to Poireiton by his elder brother Thawarel etc. So the Meitei mythology gives the impression that there was a system of sharing common wife or taking of elder brother's wife by younger brothers during the life time of the elder brother or after his death. Similar practice is found among some hill tribes of Manipur.

Last of all, a certain feature of polyandry was there in the Meitei society. As for instance low status of women (marital status), selling of wife by husband, widow by relatives or state to clear the debt etc. are indication of it.From the above facts, we cannot altogether neglect the hypothesis about the existence of polyandry system in the Meitei society before the introduction of present form.

Polygamy

The system of Polygamy was in Manipur from the very beginning of her history. The progenitors of the Moirang clan (Thangjing) had two wives, another proginator, that of Khuman clan (Wangbarel) had seven wives, so and so on. It was also prevailing custom among the Meitei that, as a symbol of success in the war, the victor took the wife of the vanquished. Again as a sort of political strategy, weak rulers or chiefs used to offer their daughter to the powerful king.Thus powerful kings had many wives or queens.

The Meitei (Ninghtouja) kings had three wives in general and they were classified as Leimaren (chief queen), Apanbi (personel favour, Vavati) Leima khubi (influential, Parivtri). Later on one more queen i.e. Apanbi naha was added to synchronise with the Hindu system.

Introduction of Hinduism in the 18th century encouraged the system of polygamy in Manipur especially in royal family. Garibaniwaj had ten queens and Bhgyachandra had ninety four. Thus each and every king after Garibaniwaj had more than four wives as permited by law. Their example was followed by the nobles and well-to-do families. So from the 18th century Polygamy became a fashion amongst the officers.

Another system of polygamy that was practised by the royal family was the system jf "Sana-mityeng-taba". Under this system, whenever the king saw a beautiful girl by chance or on any occasion, he managed to meet the girl any how and reserved her for himself. Such a girl might be left untouched throughout her life. But nobody was allowed to encroach on the king's privilege for reserving the girl. Such sort of polygamy under Sana-mityeng-taba was one of the major factors for immorality amongst the women of the state.

Hinduism brought great changes in their marriage system. The king dropped traditional custom and state law. Not only polygamy was encouraged, they started the act of immoral works viz., sexual relation with the slaves, taking of widow as queen etc. They had good number of wives. The neglected queens made secret relations with the nobles and Brahmins. The king's harem became a source of immorality in the state. Besides, Meitei kings revived outdated, primitive style of Sna-i-khaiba.

The kings' example was followed by the nobles and well-to-do persons. Thus polygamy became a fashion and was even considered an ideal amongst them. The common people who could not afford more than one wife followed the example of Krishna by the male section and that of Radha by females. The heritage is still found among the devout Manipuri Vainavas.

Polygamy and Common People

The polygamy spread from the royal families to the nobles, then to the well-to-do families, lastly to the common people. But polygamy among the common people was very few as they were economically backward in general. Polygamy was among the common people under certain circumstances viz. when a woman was issueless, having no son, turned lunatic, suffering from terrible diseases (laithung thungba and acute disease) or was completely barren or indulging in immorality etc. Under such cases, with or without the permission of the first wife, another wife used to be procured. Taking opinion was in general, if the first wife was truthful and well behaved. But suppression of a wife without any reason was against the law. The women had the right to demand Nupamamal or to confiscate all the properties of the person except a drinking jar and a piece of cloth on his loins.[1]

Even though Polygamy was in vogue, monogamy was common and considered ideal to the masses. The polygamous person was treated with hatred and contempt. In their traditional belief mention was made to take special care for impotency and need for control of free sexual union. Proverbial songs are sung even today in lai haraoba ritual. The persons who could not satisfy their thirst for sexual pleasure always demanded more and more wives and even they committed immoral act like adultery to satisfy their appetite. But women looked down upon them, with disgrace. There is a Manipuri proverb which shows their dislikes of a polygamous person.

"Puna Sangbai Natatpa"

Its literal meaning is that an old basket (Sangbai= basket used for the measure of paddy) has no handles. It means that, women dislike a person who is already married. They like a fresh and new one. Only in exceptional circumstances viz. political pressure, force, economic burden, desire of wealth, prestige and extraordinary circumstances a girl accept the position of a second or another wife of a person.

There was rarely happiness, peace and prosperity in a polygamous family. Quarrel, enmity, conspiracy, and distrust were general feature of such a family. In general, the husband gave special care and favour to the second wife whom they term as Atonbi, i.e. the last wife. Taking advantages of such favouritism, the second wife or Atonbi used to demonstrate disrespect and ill treatment to the first wife. It was very common here that, the second wife or Atonbi in order to win the favour of her husband used many devices including sorcery (Potsem jadu) which caused dislike of the first wife and ruined health of the first wife or made them suffer from lunacy etc. So Atonbi was in general bitter to all, except the husband. In some cases the first wife too made similar effort against the Atonbi. Thus there ensued a tug of war between the two wives or more which ultimately led to the downfall of the family and misfortune of the husband. In most cases the first wife left the house and retired to her parent's house. So Polygamy in Manipur was a dangerous family war.

Adultary

The case of adultery was very rare as the punishment to adulterer was very severe. The state had a special court for women.i.e. "Pacha Loishang" to deal with all the cases relating to woman, viz. adultery, insult, beating, divorce, etc. A heavy fine was imposed on the adulterer to meet the bride price and it was given to the husband of the woman. The court also took a share. In the 19th century the amount of fine (Nupi mamal) was fixed to rupees 50 (fifty) and the share for court was rupees five only.[2] Really it was a heavy fine. If the offender was not able to pay the said fine he himself along with his family was seized and sold as slaves to the satisfaction of the claiment. Both the male and female offenders were arrested and confined until the claim was satisfied, after which they were free. Besides the general form of punishment, we find cases of banishment (both the male and female), exposing to the bazar (khongaoinaba), to make blindness and mutilation of manhood in extraordinary cases.[3] So, there was no hard and fast rule for the punishment, it depended on the will of the judges. In some cases the women who w as involved in adultery was either excommunicated or divorced.

The woman who was involved in adultery was either excommunicated or divorced. Sometimes if the women were found guilty, she was banished. Some husband used to cut the hair of his wife, instead of taking helps of law court. But it seems that Manipuris /(Meiteis) were not in the favour of such women.

Factors for the Selection of Partners

There were different factors for the selection of a mate. Exogamy was the common feature of their marriage. Anyone who married a girl of his clan was deprived of many privileges viz, deprives from Pibaship if eligible, forbidden in all religious works, debarred from state jobs etc. So, the first thing for the selection of a mate was to see whether the girl was within her clan (Yek thoknaba). As there were seven clans among the community, the rules gave no hindrances in procuring a wife from other clans. Strict norms were observed later on and those culprits were exiled.

The second important factor for choosing a girl was caste. It is generally believed that, the system of caste was brought in Mariipur by Hindus in the 18th century A.D. But actually the heresy of caste was there in the land from time immemorial. But it is very interesting that, marriage with the low caste people was there in those days under certain restrictions. To cite a few examples, Konthoujam lairembi was taken as wife by one Sorarel (Tari) who belong to a higher class. In that case the woman was forbidden to go and dine with her family and other clan members of her own. On one occasion she was forced to take meal with her family accordingly, she was expelled by her husband. On another occasion, Nongda Lairen Pakhangba took Laishna, as one of his wives, but the former lived together with her only during the night. On querry, Nongda told her that, he belonged to the god clan, while Laishna belonged to namu-taibang mee hence, they couldn't live together openly on social ground.[4] From the above facts, it seems that, taking of wife from the low caste section was considered a social degradation.

There were three major ethinic groups or caste viz. Lai, Mee and Teen.[5] The Lai section claimed themselves as higher caste. Such casteheresy was continued upto 17th century A.D. which was completely abolished by king Khagemba (17th century A.D.). But Hindunisation in the 18th century A.D. once more brought the system of caste. Marriage with the low caste people like Ganak, Haram people and tribal people or non-Hindu were either outcasted or punished with exilement. Contrary to it a non Brahmin person who took Brahmin women also got the same fate. Progenitors of the Manipuri Brahmin took tribal, Loi, Meitei and Muslim women as their wife. 'Accordingly outsiders treated Manipuri Brahmin as caste Brahmin on account of their impure blood. Other minor factors for choosing a partner were beauty, character, status, economy and love.

Love marriage or marriage by personel intimacy was a common form of marriage even today. As stated above the parents permitted the children to choose their own partner to avoid the complaint in future. In such form of becoming husband and wife, the boy and girl by their personel intimacy or love made the elopement and the parent made arrangement for marriage i.e it was solemnized by the ritual of Luhongba, Keinya katpa or Loukhatpa according to their convinences. So,the general form of marriage among the Meiteis was love marriage through elopement and solemnized by Luhongba, 80% of the population performed such system of marriage.

Most of the respondents pointed out that, love marriage is the best, according to their opinion, the relation between a husband and wife is not a nightmare, and the tie is for the whole life. So it will be a wise step to choose a partner having close intimacy, to know the character of the mate by a close watch of long companionship. In their opinion marriage leads to a peaceful and co operation in their family life even though they may meet many odd things in their life, tackle the problems with patience. So, love is not blind among the Meiteis. The only problem which arises in the present society is breach of social restrictions like Yek thoknaba, Mungnaba and caste bar. In the love marriage the partners generally neglected the factors like beauty, character, status etc. which was duely taken into account in engagement. In spite of all these the value of marriage by engagement cannot be treated lightly and some are being proud of having such type of marriage.

Above all, the parents considered it their bounden duty to choose or have a good daughter in- law of their own son. According to their religious belief, the daughter will be the mother of the next life. So, they expected a good Mou (daughter in law) even though they left the matter to their son to escape from future complaints.

Dowry

The system of giving Dowry on limited scale was common in Manipur both among the hills and plain peoples, but it was not compulsory as we find in India. Probably, the Meitei followed Kachin or Maru culture in this respect. Only the greedy person or parents try to choose bride from rich family on the expectation of a good dowry. The girls used to prepare themselves all the necessary clothes for their marriage and took them as dowry. The parents, if affordable gave some more articles at the time of marriage or at the time of Loukhatpa. There was no objection from the side of the groom and family regarding the quantity of dowry. But the women who brought a good dowry lived respectably in the family.

Divorce

The marital relation between man and woman in the early days was not as strong as in the present days. There was no hard and first rule to deal with divorce. It has already been mentioned that, women were very free and even they left her husband home and made union with other person and once more returned to the family. But that was the case of pre-christian era. But with the beginning of Christian era a court dealing with the case of women-Divorce, quarrel, adultery, beating of women etc were set up during the reign of Nogda Lairen Pakhangba (1st century A.D.)

Women were treated as the property of husband, probably it was due to taking of huge bride price. R. Brown pointed out that, the husband sold the wife and children for debt and even for the purchase of a horse.[6] Such slave women can be enjoyed by the master whenever desired so and the children born became the property of the master. If it was really true, the position of a housewife was very low and it was a shameful custom of the community. We find the same custom among the Chins. Whenever the husband became displeased with his wife, the latter could be turned out at will by giving false charges. If the women was in pregnancy or having a small child in her arms, the person was liable to bear the foods of the children (Angang chakthak) but nothing could be claimed by the women, except her dowry. Other factors of divorce were issuelessness, having no son, becoming lunartic, suffering from terrible disease (laithung thungba), complete barreness or indulging in immorality. But unreasonable divorce was not permitted. The matter can be placed before Pacha Loishang and the court may permit to confiscate all the properties of the person except a cloth on his Loins.

A housewife was respected if she was able to produce a male issue or brought a good dowry or had a good number of relatives (Khukan panganba). A woman who became a housewife under proper norm of marriage and bore male issue first got many social privileges. Otherwise a housewife was generally looked down upon. So, some of them lived in a miserable condition not better than a slave. Even though they insisted on their not returning as far as possible as it was against the custom of Meiteis. No married women should die in the parent's house. Again their brother in law also did not like to take the risk of the sister and her children. The sister also knew the sentiment of the brothers etc. So some women passed their days in their husband's house in a very miserable condition.

Marriage and its Forms

To become husband and wife was known as Yum-panba. The proper ritual which solemnized the tie was known as Luhongba. But the name itself was abridged from the word 'Nu-hongba' (Nu=Penis?), Hongba^ plenty i.e. free availability of penis). Without performing the ritual of Luhongba a couple might became husband and wife through some limited rituals viz. (1) Keinya katpa, and (2) Loukhatpa. There were also cases of becoming husband and wife without having any sort of solemnization. Some orthodox family refused to take the" food cooked by such women. Not only their social status was low, but certain priviledges were not given to those women who did not perform Luhongba. So, the ritual which accepted a person as husband or wife may broadly be devided into three viz. (1) Luhongba, (20 Keinya katpa, and (3) Loukhatpa.

There were different means of becoming husband and wife viz. (1) Arrangement by the parents or relatives (Haina-singnaduna luhongba), (2) choosing by themselves and making an elopement (chenba) and (3) to take forcibly (chingba). Whatever might be the method, the tie was solemnized by one of the above three rituals viz. Luhongba or Keinya katpa or Loukhatpa according to their conveniences. The system is still in practice.

Preparation for Marriage

There were four processes in engagement for a marriage. They were (1) Nupi haiba (go between) (2) Yathangthaba, (3) Waroipot puba, and (4) Heijingkharai puba.

Nupihaiba

In traditional Meitei society in the preparation for marriage, there was go between. An emissary led by some friends or relatives of the family was sent along with some presentation like cloth, flower, fruits, sweetmeat and pan. In general i t was done by an expert woman, who reported to the elders of the family (family of the expected bride) for the marriage. But in some novels like Nugbal pombi luwaoba the mother herself took the role of emissary. In some folk tales, the father does the same work. So it seems that there was no hard and fast rule in this matter. It depended upon their convinences and the mode of relation between the two families.

If an arrangement was brought the marriage was held sooner or later on an auspicious day. But in some cases even though the proposal was accepted, the date of marriage was not exactly fixed. Rather it was decided tentatively to perform the marriage after a few months or years. The delay was mainly to improve economic condition of the family of the bride as it involved the question of dowry or to attain maturity of the couple or the bride or to keep watchful eyes upon the groom and his family etc. So after the stipulated period, the proposal might be rejected, if they found it unsatisfactory. Another type of go between was mutual arrangement between the two friends or families to give into marriage and expected children in the womb when they would attain maturity as a token of love. In some cases, their arrangement was strengthened by a promise. But in most cases such promises was not kept at all, when one of the parties became fortunate or when there was no cordial relation between the two families. But there was no trace of child marriage. During the early period the age of marriage for girl was 13 to 15 and for boys it was 16 to 18,. if the marriage was in pending under the second or third type of arrangement, the family of the groom used to present cloths for the prospective bride either annually or on all festive occasions.

Yathang Thaba

The first step in preparation of a marriage was go between. It was followed by the process of Yathangthaba, which literally means to give formal order for the marriage. When the parents of the girl agreed to give the hands of their daughter, the father used to express his desire in the form of a declaration. The process was known as Yathangthaba. After this, the family of the groom started preparation for the marriage and the date of Waroipot and Heijing Kharai puba was fixed.

Waroipot Puba

The third step in the preparation of marriage was Waroipot puba when the final decision for the marriage was made to the bride's family. The presentation comprises cloths, fruits, pan, sweets, etc. The articles were offered to their ancestral deities and partaken of together. For the royal and well to do families, the ceremony was performed on a large scale. There are some modifications in their preparation of marriage. Nowadays waroipot was preceded the Heijing kharai puba (Heijapot). The folk tales of Moirang (Khamba-Thoibi) and Tampha lairembi of Wangoo clearly indicate it. In those early days, the marriage ceremony was delayed for many months after the event of Heijing kharai puba. So no final decision was arrived at only after Heijing Kharai Puba. The old system of supplying cotton and iron (iron bars) for the preparation of cloths and necessary weapons is almost neglected. A piece of cotton and iron have substituted for the old practice. Similarly, supplying of cotton and bean- seeds by the bride's family is also almost neglected. Modernisation has brought all these changes.

Heijing Kharai Puba

The last process in the preparation of marriage was Heijing kharai puba. It was a second presentation made to the bride's family on an auspicious day by the groom's family and brought by the local elders in Phingaruks and trays (Lukmais) full of Kabok(puffed rice mixed with molasses), fruits, pan, sweets-and others in a procession to the bride's family. Certain fruits viz., Heikru and Heining were compulsory, in case of unavialibility, their leaves or stems substituted for them. The procession was very pictureqe, women in fine traditional costume carrying the baskets or trays form a procession in a long line.They were received warmly by the bride's family. As in the previous case, the articles were offered to their ancestral Gods viz. ancestor of the clan and sub clan, Sanamahi, local and guardian gods. Then articles were distributed and consumed. Even though the system of Heijing kharai puba was following the heritage of mythical Tampha Lairembi, it was a kind of party held to express their joy for the marriage. They also informed their ancestral spirits and begged for blessings. At the same time, the ceremony forecast the reservation of the girls as the wife of the suitor. After this occasion, no suitor was permitted. The first suitor had the right to claim all the expenses so far made in connection with the preparation of the marriage or Nupimamal.

Luhongba

When all the preparation was over, the date of the marriage was fixed on an auspicious day. The marriage was performed at the residence of the bride. The groom in a procession led by some women carrying the bride price or Kujaba, Chiruk nungshang, a basket full of fruits and pan to be offered to the ancestral gods, came to the residence of the bride accompanied by a musical party. The groom was received by mother or aunt of the bride after passing a fire kindled to drive out evil-spirits (dihuti okpa, maya okpa). Then the marriage was started if there arose no objection to the bride price or Kujaba. The marriage itself was divided into two viz. (1) marriage performed with full ritual and (2) marriage performed under a limited ritual.

Niyom Chumna Hongba Luhongba (Marriage which is Performed with full Ritual)

The process for such type of marriage was a lengthy one. The main item of the ceremony was to solemnized the tie by sacrificial ritual either by the kindling of fire (Mei-latpa) or installation of water pot (Iratphu latpa). It was followed by some minor items viz. Kujaba punba (tying of bride's palm with that of the groom), Lei koiba (going round the groom by the bride with flowers), Hukpa (wreathing the neck of the groom with a garland of flowers), Kangshubi lanba (passing over of sweets made of til), etc. In the marriage ceremony of the Meiteis, the blessings of the ancestral spirits was sought and they were informed about the inclusion of a new member to the sagei by offering fruits, pan, sweets, etc, etc. Along with it, omen was also sought through Chiruk nungshang and Ngamu thaba (setting free of the mud fish in the water). Thus there were different items in their marriage ceremony. The ceremony was concluded by a grand feast (mapam Chakouba) on the sixth day of the ceremony.

Niyom Chumna Hongdaba Luhongtia Marriage with limited Rituals

The second type of marriage was designed specially for those women, who had eloped and spent one night or more without any restriction, or kidnapped women, or a women who was not previously married but was a wife of someone. If such women wanted to perform marriage, they were permitted to do so without observing sacrificial rite i.e. mei-latpa and iratphu latpa. Other items were the same.

It is doubtful that the said system of marriage performance with sacrificial rites was the outcome of Hindu influence. Again there were different views about the original form of marriage system in the traditional Meitei society. All these views cannot be neglected altogether from the fact that the ancestors of the present Meitei people belong to different ethinic groups and tribes having divergent cultures and habits. So we find the heritage of the Thais (Southern Thais), the black Tais, the Kha (Cheh race) etc. But inspite of all these diversities, the early marriage system was simple and sort. Ancestral spirits were summoned and informed of the inclusion of the new member and their blessings was sought. The couple bent down before the spirits of the ancestors at least three times as a sign of veneration. Its heritage is still found in the 'Laitin thaba'. Such system of marriage is still practised among the Black Tais. As regard the abode of the spirits some section took it in the south western corner of the room where the marriage ceremony was performed. The two garlands made of white flowers (Kundo) were offered to the deity and then the couple put on the garlands by themselves in turn. But no accurate account is available about their early marriage system.

Keinya Katpa

It was a simple form of betrothal ceremony. It was a very common form of solemnizing a tie specially in the rural areas and among poor people. Not only the procedure of the betrothal was very simple, and short but also less expensive. So, common people who could not afford the expenses of the marriage and dowry arranged the marriage of their daughter by the system of Keinya katpa. On the other hand the system allowed a man and women to be husband and wife though the women was not permitted to perform marriage specially for Cheluraba nupi (eloped or kidnapped girls) or Mou (married women). The system of Keinya katpa was also very simple. Two garlands were offered to Lainingthou Sanamahi and put on the necks of the couple by themselves in the front of their parents and elders present, then they bowed their heads before the ancestral gods and Sanamahi and members present on the occasion. The articles which which were brought by the groom's family were offered to the deities viz. Sanamahi, ancestral gods, and Lam lais or the guardian gods. It was then distributed and consumed. The ceremony was concluded by offering a meal to the new couple by the family of the bride in the evening or another day. In the case of adultery, if the culprit is ever caught he was forced to take the woman by performing Keinya katpa and forced to pay nupimamal (bride price to the husband).

Loukhatpa

Another simple form of betrothal was Loukhatpa. A couple might become husband and wife without performing either Luhongha or Keinya katpa but by the ritual of Loukhatpa. The meals for the marriage ceremony (Mapam chak-kouba) and for Keinya katpa were also a part of this ritual. Failing which, the bride was excommunicated by her parents and some orthodox in laws refused to take food cooked by her. She was also forbidden to enter the house of her parents.

The ceremony of Loukhatpa was applicable only to those who became husband and wife by elopement or by kidnap against the wishes of the parents. For many reasons they were excommunicated without performing any ritual. But later on a formal recognisation was given to them by the ritual of Loukhatpa. The process of Loukhatpa was almost the same *as* Keinya Katpa. Here, only the garland putting was omitted. Giving of dowry was also common in the Loukhatpa and Keinya katpa ceremony. But in general the amount was less.

The system of Keinya Katpa and Loukhatpa are still in practice in the Meitei society. Recognition of husband and wife was compulsory in the traditional Meitei society. So, there was the case of Loukhatpa after five or ten years later. Sometimes it was done by relatives as her parents refused to do so. Traditional system of marriage and its different kinds viz. Keinya Katpa and Loukhatpa have common feature in the southern Thai and black Tai with some local variations. The process of Sanskritisation in the 18th century A.D. had its impact on the traditional system of marriage.

Hindu ritual was added and traditional rite was substituted for by Hindu rite but the features of the ceremony remained unchanged. In the Keinya katpa and Loukhatpa rituals, Brahmin porohit was employed. The present style of dress in marriage was the influence of Hindunisation in the 18th century A.D.

In the traditional Meitei society there were different style of becoming husband and wife. They were (1) Haina Shingnaba (go between), (2) Chenba (elopement), (3) Chingba (Kidnapped), (4) Nambo thaba (Persuation).

In the case of Haina Shingnaba the arrangement was made by the parents or relatives as discussed earlier. But in the case of chenba, the couple either by mutual agreement or love between themselves became husband and wife. But in extra ordinary cases, the parents also arranged the marriage ceremony or to avoid misfortunes.

The third type of becoming husband and wife i.e. chingba was forcible taking of a girl as a wife by means of kidnap. As there evolved the question of prestige and problem of future marriage, the girl in general accepted such forcible inducement. The last type of becoming husband and wife is an interesting one when a boy failed in any sort of attempt to win the hands of a girl, the system of Nambothaba was adopted as last attempt. The boy along with a huge bundle containing various articles (nambo) used to come to the house of the girl and asked for the girl's hands. He took a seat in the Sangoi of the family and worked for the family as a member until and unless the girl agreed to give her hands. It was a kind of persuasion as if it were the hunger-strike for love's sake.

According to Chaki Sirchar. in most cases the boy was beaten black and blue by the brothers of the girl and driven out of the family. If the boy was stubborn, the village elders came to his support. Sometimes the parents were attracted by the attitude of the boy and they induced their daughter to accept the marriage. Similarly the girl was also attracted by the boy and she began to love the boy. Such a case mostly happened in the family having no son and the boy became an adopted son-in-law.(Yaong inba).

Bride Price (Nupimamal)

The system of offering bride price was vogue in the Meitei society from the very early period. The price was usually returned in the case of divorce and the same was given in the form of fine in case of adultery. No accurate amount was fixed about the bride price, but it seems that, the price was very heavy as prevalent among the surrounding hill tribes. In the early days the bride price generally included a pair of bullocks, cloths, ornaments for the bride etc, but later on cash payment was introduced probably Rs. 50/- in the 19th century A.D. The system of giving bride price is completely dropped in the urban areas now a day. But the amount of bride price depends upon their mutual agreement. The money so taken was used for the preparation of dowry and other expenses of the marriage. Nowadays the money has been substituted for by some presentation to the bride.

Mangkat

It was a kind of fee given to the family of the groom by the bride's family. The purpose of the fee was admission to the burial or cremation ground of the groom's family by the bride. So, a woman if divorce and not married to another person, was brought to the burial of cremation ground of her husband or family. The dead woman was send out to her family or parents. In the royal family the rate of fee was very high. Besides the money, they used to give different presentation viz. Cloths, fruits, sweets, pan, etc. But the rate of the free for common people is not known As in. Bride price, here also the fee was agreed upon a coin.

Bride Price (Nupimamal)

The system of offering bride price was vogue in the Meitei society from the very early period. The price was usually returned in the case of divorce and the same was given in the form of fine in case of adultery. No accurate amount was fixed about the bride price, but it seems that, the price was very heavy as prevalent among the surrounding hill tribes. In the early days the bride price generally included a pair of bullocks, cloths, ornaments for the bride etc, but later on cash payment was introduced probably Rs. 50/- in the 19th century A.D. The system of giving bride price is completely dropped in the urban areas now a day. But the amount of bride price depends upon their mutual agreement. The money so taken was used for the preparation of dowry and other expenses of the marriage. Nowadays the money has been substituted for by some presentation to the bride.

Mangkat

It was a kind of fee given to the family of the groom by the bride's family. The purpose of the fee was admission to the burial or cremation ground of the groom's family by the bride. So, a woman if divorce and not married to another person, was brought to the burial of cremation ground of her husband or family. The dead woman was send out to her family or parents. In the royal family the rate of fee was very high. Besides the money, they used to give different presentation viz. Cloths, fruits, sweets, pan, etc. But the rate of the free for common people is not known As in. Bride price, here also the fee was agreed upon a coin.

Khul-Wa-Kongba

The family of the groom used to pay a presentation or certain money to the villagers for seeking the permission of the marriage. The elders of the village arranged a party by the money so taken.

It was common in certain Chakpa villages to provide Yu (intoxicated liquor) to the villagers and have a good party. Nowadays in some rural areas, Jatra-wali is arranged at the residence of the bride or village ground and the expense is borne by the groom's family. So Khul Wa-Kongba was a kind of social get together and enjoyment.

Thangja Phi-Yen

Matrimonial alliance with the royal families viz. Rajkumar, Maharajkumar and their indirect descendents (Taibungo/ Leima) was very expensive, some additional presentation and fee like Thangja Phi-yen and Kwagok Hanba were compulsory in their case. Both the parties used to present at least a piece of cloth (Pheijom or Khudei) to all the elders and married persons of the Sageis. But in most cases the presentation was restricted only to elders and parents. Such type of presentation was known as Thanja Phi-yen.

Kwagok Hanba

In all the cases of matrimonial alliance with the royal families, a sum of money known as Kwagok hanba used to be paid by common people. When a commoner took a wife from the royal family or gave a daughter to the royal family, the said fee was compulsory. In reality it was a fee for having matrimonial alliance with the royal family and for the priviledge of acquiring the title of Taibungo or Angang and Sija. During 19th and early 20th century no person was able to get any high post of the state, unless he married a woman of the royal family. The system of Kwagok hanba and Thangja Phi-yen is still in practice in the Meitei society but on a limited scale. The chronicles mention the demand of one slave for the marriage with royal family.

Marriage Rules

There were certain prescriptive marriage rules in the traditional Meitei society. They reckon blood relationship with both the male and female lines. Accordingly, their rules were of patrilineal and matrilineal kinds, thereby indicating the existence of a kind of double consanguineous kinship system. Important rules were Yek-thoknaba or Pu-tinnaba, Sairuk tinnaba, Pentinaba and Mungnaba.

Yek Thoknaba

The Meiteis were exogamous people. Marriage within the clan or Yek was strictly prohibited. Such restrictions were known as Yek-thoknaba i.e. having consanguineous kinship. It was believed that, each and every clan (Yek/ Salai) had common ancestor or Pu (the great grandfather). So Yek thoknaba was also known as Pu-tinnaba. Their rule was specially based on blood relationship. The present rule of Yek- tho k naba was based on consanguineous kinship traced from patrilineal side. But just before the introduction of the present system during the 'Salai' periods, there was the trace of endogamous marriage system. Khaba Shokchromba alias Leirenhan the father in law of Panthoibai married a woman (Manutengacha) from his own clan (Khaba).[7] Such system was found among the local hill tribes of Manipur like Kom (an old Kuki tribe). But the rule of Yek thoknaba was not applicable to those 'Yeks' of the Haram people. Their Yek was only given for their identity. By way of example, the marriage between two Yumnaks of Ningthoujam, one of the indegeneous clan and the other from Lairik Yengbam lol (westerner), was permitted even though they belonged to the same Yek i.e. Ninghouja. The two are not bound by the rule of consanguineal kinship. But the outsiders or members of other clans, ever affiliated permanently under the rule of Yokchaba (adopted), followed the rule of clan exogamy i.e. yek-thoknaba.

Sairuk-Tinnaba

Like the system of Yek-thoknaba, the patrilineal consanguineal kinship was extended in their inter clan context too. Princes born to the same clan occasionally left their clan and got affiliated to another clan (Yek), while some remained in the clan of their origin. The same was there among the common people. Under the rule of Yek-thoknaba such children were permitted to have matrimonial with different Yek. But the rule of Sairuk tinnaba prohibited the said relation. Amongst the royal families, the restriction was operated by the rule of Shairuk Achouba, and the prohibitation was forever. But the cases of commcn people were guided by the rule of Sairuk Macha and the restriction was for a limited period of only two generations. There were only four groups of Sairuk- Achouba and a number of Sairuk Macha.[8]

Pen-Tinnaba

Along with the patrilineal form of Kinship relation, Meitei also followed the rule of matrilineal consanguineal Kinship. Such kinship relation, traced from the matrilineal side, was known as Pen-tinnaba. As in the case of Sairuk tinnaba, the rule of Pen tinnaba was also divided into two categories, viz. (1) Leinung- pen tinnaba and (2) New Pentinnaba or Pi-tinnaba.

Leinung Pentinnaba was a kind of kin relationship holding between the descendents belonging to two or more exogamous clans, yet if a woman married to more than one husband of different clans her children born to them were affiliated to different clans. Such children were restricted in their marital relation. As in the case of Sharuk-Achouba there also in the case of Leinung pen-tinnaba, there were six cases of unique primeval historical formation. The restriction was also forever.

The rule of new pentinnba or pi-tinnaba was more or less similar to Shairuk macha but based on matrilineal kins. But it was the case of individual persons. By the way of example, two or more children having common mother but having different fathers might be affiliated to different clans. Matrilineal relation of such children was prohibited for two generations.[9]

So in strict sense the rule of Pen-tinnaba was more or less similar to Shairuk tinnaba. The former was based on matrilineal kinship and the later on patrilineal system.

Mungnaba (Cross Cousin Marriage)

Another prescriptive marriage rule of the traditional Meitei society was the rule of Mungnaba. The rule was devided into three categories according to the mode of its application. They were-(l) manem matung inba, (2)

Mingouna yaba, and (3) Ningol macha masel lounaba yadaba.The first and second type were the forms of cross-cousin marriage. The first one was the form of matrilineal cross cousin marriage and the last one was the form of maternal parallel cross cousin marriage. The system of cross cousin marriage was considered as ideal. The honorary titles of Sanamahi and Tamphasana were given to the children born to them. But in reality it was against the rule of Shairuk and Pendinlol. The system was dropped altogether from the 19th century A.D., probably owing to influence of the Brahmins and the rule of Mungnaba was adopted. It meant that the rule forbidding the cross cousin marriage came to be known as Mungnaba.

In the case of the third type of norms, the children of the two sisters married to different clans or Sageis, were considered to have blood relation through their mothers or grand mother. Matrilineal relation among such children was restricted by the rule of Mungnaba. The rule of I-mungnaba or Mungnaba was in force only for five generations. But if their children crossed different Sageis through marriage, the rule was inoperative.

Conclusion

The tie for husband and wife requires a solemnization by a ritual viz. Luhongba, Keinya katpa and Loukhatpa. Their marriage system was the prototype of southern Thais and Black Tais, with some local variation. Again the rule of marriage was based on both patrilineal and matrilineal kinship and was applied only in the inter clan context. This shows existence of the two systems side by side in different parts on the country and suppression of the matrilineal society by the patrilineal. In the opinion of Dr.Ch. Budhi Singh, the present system is very much akin to proto sino Tibetian and matrilineal kinship system was of later penetration. But in reality matrilineal society preceded over the patrilineal here.

Again the present system of marriage was the outcome of Hindunisation which owed its origin from the last quarter of 18th century or 1st quarter of the 19th century A.D. The exact form of marriage in those days is in mystery. Probably Meitei followed Black Thai system. Hindunisation also added new rules of marriage giving emphasis on matrilineal Kinship system.

REFERENCES

1. T.C. Hodson.TheMeitheis.p. 91.
2. Ibid.
3. N. Birachandra singh :- Socio-religious life of the Meiteis in the 18lh century. A.D.(Ph.D. thesis), p. 116-17.
4. N. Indramani Singh. Pakhangba Laihui. p. 26-27.
5. K. Chandrasekhar. Loiyumba Shilyan, p. 48.
6. T.C.Hodson-opcit, p. 91.
7. M. Chandra Singh. - Panthoiba Khongul, p. 35.
8. I-tinaba & Pen-tinnaba-Unpublished M.S.
9. Ibid.

CHAPTER THREE

PRE-HINDUNISATION BETROTHAL CEREMONY OF THE MEITEIS

Pre-Hindunisation Betrothal Ceremony

It is not an easy task to give a vivid picture of the betrothal ceremony of the Meiteis before Hindunisation. According to Colonel Mecullock,for becoming husband and wife, the ritual of marriage was not compulsory among the Meiteis.[1] In their society an unmarried person, both the husband and wife was not only looked down upon, but also certain priviledges were not given. As for instance, she was not allowed to participate in all important religious and social functions. She can not lead the marriage procession i.e. Jatra puba, so also the person and his sons were not getting many priviledges. Such a person was forbidden to serve as a royal bodyguard. (Ningthou senba). Piba of the sagei etc. Accordingly they used to perform marriage ceremony as far as possible. No doubt, the purpose of marriage is to take permission and evidences of the public for union.But in the Meitei custom, there was elements of religious sanctity, specially to give information to their ancestral gods and ancestors (three ancestors in acending order, Purol ahum) and begging for their blessing. So, the ritual of Lai-tin thaba was compulsory. In the betrothal ceremony under Keinya Katpa and Loukhatpa, the ritual of lai-tin thaba forms its main items.

Go-between (Haina singnaba)

There was certain formality of go between in a marriage. At present the family of the groom use to gives presentation for three times to the family of the bride by the Loi community and four times by the Meiteis. The system was described as Yukhom Ahumlak thaba. (Sending wine three times) by Loi community of the Manipur. For them the presentation was made by Yu (Alcohol). But among the Meitei the article varies according to its occasion i.e. first approach, Yathang thaba, Heiching Kharaipuba and Wariopot. In the early Christian era and prior to that, there were only two occasions of giving presentation in the go between for marriage. In the first occasion fruits, bunches of flowers (Leinachom) were given as presentations.[2] But in the case of Panthoibi mention is made of inclusion of coins.[3] If the girl accepted the proposal she took the fruits and put the flowers on her ear. Again if the parent too agreed to give the hands of their daughter they would invite for Heiching-Karai-Puba. Now adays a second ceremony known as Yathang thaba i.e. announcement for giving the hands of their daughter is also observed which is followed by Waroipot. The groom's house brought sweets. Pan, fruits etc. and it is offered to ancestral gods and local gods and it is consumed by the members present. After the occasion, the bride is reserved for the groom and new approach was not accepted.

Heiching-Karai-Puba

The word Heiching Kharai owed its origin from the words Haija-pot which literally means articles for request (presentation for request). The main function on that day was to present a tray made of bamboo containing different items of fruits by the groom's father to the father of the bride at the residence of the latter.The party of groom family arriving in a procession carrying the articles of presentations in a long row is a picturesque spectacle. On that day the matter of bride price and Kwagokhanba, if required would be settled.

In the early Christian era, the articles for Heiching karai consisted of the baskets of rice, fish, salt, fruits, two pots of intoxicating liquor.Heikru and Heining (Gooseberry & Hog fruit) were compulsory. It is said that, on the occasion of Heiching Kharai Puba of Tampha lairembi, the two fruits were left out, hence the enraged goddess cursed the procession party of the groom's family to become stone statues.[4] From that occasion onward the two fruits became compulsory and even though the fruits are not available they used to add a stem or leaf of the fruits. A bullock and a slave served the purpose of bride price.[5] But for the Ningthouja clans and Mangang, buffalo and a slave were given as bride price.[6] We can't get an accurate account about the bride price of the common people. The bride price among the hill tribes was very high. But among the Meiteis the rate was the cost of a slave. In all the cases of refundment of bride price and fine for adultery the rate was fixed at the rate of a slave i.e. Rs 50/- in the 19th century AD.[7] But according to some scholars the rate varies on mutual agreement between the two parties which may be fixed even on a coin. Some are of the opinion that,if the groom's family was not in a position to pay the bride price in full the groom might be induced to stay and work for a few years at the residence of the father in law. Thus there arises the case of Yaong inba.

There is no fixed date for Haiching karai puba, it is usually performed one or two days ahead of the marriage ceremony. Generally, it is performed on an auspicious day.

As stated above, on this day the case of bride price was also settled. Now adays in the Imphal area the bride price is substituted by a presentation to the bride known as Kujaba. The articles comprises one Phanek (lower garment of the women) Mapal naiba made of pure muga (phige phanek mapal naiba) and chaddar made of muga (phijil chalba enaphi) .These articles are shown on the day of Heiching Kharaipuba.

Heiching kharai puba/presentation ceremony of Heiching kharai can be made on the day of marriage from the fact that, in the marriage ceremony of Melnu the daughter of king Yoimongba of Ningthouja clan with Sararel of Angom clan the latter brought the Heiching Kharai on the very day of the marriage. Some scholars of the opinion that, the present system as stated above came into existence after some modification for the convinences of the parties to avoid overburden and quarrel for bride price etc. From the above fact and figures the Heiching kharai presentation can be made on any convinent date, even on the day of marriage or earlier. There were no hard and fast rules.

Betrothal Ceremony

On the day of marriage the bridegroom along with his party arrived at the residence of the bride along with some specific articles. The groom was received by the mothers. (Mama & Mandomchas) with due ceremony. After Hindunisation a sankritan became compulsory in the marriage ceremony. So if the sankritan could not complete the item of Raga, the groom and his party have to await outside for its completion. Then the betrothal ceremony will start in the presence of both parties. The groom and bride would be seated on a mat or cloth. The bride on the left side of the groom. The right palm of the bride will be placed above the palm of the groom and it will be tied with a garland by the mother of the bride.[8] The process was known as Kujaba-Punba.

The word Kujaba literally means to give or endow i.e the hands of the bride (her daughter) to the groom. The main theme of Meitei marriage was this item of kujaba. In the present system after the performance of Kujaba punba an earthern tray containing rice, coconut, betel leaf and nut, a bunch of banana having even number, one Peijom and Khudei(lower garment of male),a knife and ceser will be placed above the plams of the two. The articles are called Kuja-pot. A purohit or expert will summon the Almighty god, three ancestors of the bride & the groom in ascending order to witness the tic, permission for the inclusion of a new member in the groom family and sub clan and begging for blessings to the new couple. The father of the bride generally offers the Kujaba. Then he will bless them with money (farel selja Kubiba) its present term is dan-thadaba. The thread and articles of Kujaba would be removed and handled over to the groom's mother.

It is generally believed that, the items of Kujaba punba and kujaba are of new addition after Hindunisation. But the system is not found in any section of Hindu community. Above all, the articles which comprise Kujaba have its deep philosophical meaning owing its origin from local concept rather than foreign.The question here is if, the system was a traditional practice or new addition and if it was a new one when it was introduced? So a further investigation is required. In my opinion, it was probably new addition in the 17th century AD before Hindunisation.

The next item of the betrothal after Kujaba was garlanding. The bride put two garlands of white flowers (Kundo pareng in general) on the neck of the groom and in turn the groom remove one of the garlands and put the same on the neck of the bride. They were assisted by helpers (Bor senaba & Keina senaba).

Then both the groom and the bride bow their heads before the audience as sign of respect. The black Tai and southern Tai did the same procedure but they bowed their head first to the ancestral gods inside the house and then to the members present.

After Hindunisation new items were added in their marriage ceremony. Before the garlanding stated above, the bride went around the groom seven times and would throw flowers over the head of the groom for every turn of completion for six times and in the last turn the garland was put on the neck of the groom. Then the cloths of the groom and bride were fastened together and they went inside the house of the bride and presented pan and Kangshubi (se same/ til) to each other and friends. Another great impact of Hindunisation was in the dress of the marriage especially for the bride. A new lower garment known as Potloi which was specially used in the rasha dance began to be introduced as the dress of the bride from the last quarter of the 18th century AD. Prior to that the bride used Phanek mapal naiba as lower garment, Kajenglei, langmei and Shmji huk as head dresses.[9]

Conclusion

To conclude, the primitive system of marriage among the Meiteis before Hindunisation was the outcome of gradual development. It may be divided into two stages 1) Early Christian era.2) later periods from 17th to early 18th century AD.In the early stage* the betrothal ceremony was very simple. Garlanding by theseselves before the members present and bowing of head to the audience. In the second stage, the item of Kujaba punba was added. But the items of omen seeking, and information to the ancestral gods, local deities etc were the same. Again Meitei system was quite different from that of the other tribes viz. Chakpas, Kotha etc which is suggested by some local scholars. Rather, their system is more akin to black Tai.

Sending off of the Bride to the Residence of the Groom

After the end of the marriage ceremony the bride was sent to the residence of the groom immediately on the day. But there is some discrepancy regarding the sending off of the bride. In the chronicles viz Panthoibi khongul and Kouburel khungun (kouburel)mentions are made of sending of the bride on the day of marriage.But in some chronicles like Nongpal Pombi Luwaoba the bride was brought by her relatives at the residence of the Nungpal Pombi Luwaoba after some months.[10] The exact text of the book runs thus "on one month , from the residence of Koupa his daughter Namoinu samte Leinaopi was brought to the residence of Nungpal by inhabitants of Koupa along along with huge dowry. Hence the Nungpal awaited them". So the text gives an inference that the bride was send off at the residence of the groom after a few months. Among some groups of Meities who were now living outside Manipur specially in Tripura, there is now prevalent the custom of sending off the bride at the residence of the groom after five days. There is a doubt that, the Meities (Ningthouja) too followed the same custom in the early Christian era; from the fact that, when the king Yoimongba agreed to give the hands of his daughter- Melnu to the king of Angom the latter was advised to wait for five days at his residence. But actually on that occasion the bride was sent off on the very day of marriage. From the above accounts it may be assumed that, the custom differs from one clan to another. In general the bride was sent off to the residence of the groom on the very day of marriage. After the formation of a unified Meitei Kingdom, the Meitei Kings tried at their best level to introduce a uniform culture in the state.

Yaong-inba-

An interesting aspect in becoming husband and wife among the Meitei in the early periods was the custom of yaonginba i.e to live at the residence of the bride by the groom. In the matrilineal society of Khasi of Meghalaya, the groom generally lived at the residence of the bride. Among the tribes of Manipur the groom-lived at the residence of the bride for a limited period from 3 to 4 years in general from the date of marriage. Similar practices were there among the Meitei of Kotha. After the expiry of time they return to the residence of the groom. But the system of yaonginba among the hill tribe might be a forcible inducement for their inability to pay the bride price rather than a custom. The bride price among the hill tribes was very high which can hardly be paid by those economically backward people of the hills peoples of those days. So the father in law induced them to live and work for him for 3 to 4 years to recover the bride price in full or partially in the form of labour. In course of time it became a general custom in marriage. In comparision with the hill tribes, the bride price among the Meiteis was very low. For the royal family it was a pair of bullocks in general,. But for the Ningthouja clan it was the cost of a slave. It was agreed upon a coin. Nowadays it was substituted by a fixed presentation called Nupigi-Kujaba (presentation).

Unlike the hill people there was no hard and fast rules for yaonginba in the plain. The custom of yaonginba was prevalent among the Meities (Ningthouja). The Meitei King Naothingkhong left the capital and lived at the residence of his wife Nongmai Petanga at Nongmaiching before he became king of Ningthouja clan. But some scholars are of the opinion that he did so, as he had no hope of becoming the king after his father's death. The custom of Yaonginba was mostly found in the matrilineal society as stated above. With the advent of Christian era patrilineal form of society became very active in the state leading to a set-back to matrilineal one. Father became the head of the family and his power and prestiges increased, side by side the position of a housewife lowered down at its low ebb and they were even treated as slave of the husband in strict sense. So, the custom of Yaoinba began to be considered as disgraceful and was dropped gradually. But its heritage is still found in the Meitei society. The conditions to accept Yaonginba may be under the following reasons. 1) Inability to pay bride price, 2) sonless father-in-law induce the groom to live at his residence. 3) Some women due to certain reasons like, quarrel with the in laws and other members of the family took away the husband to her residence. 4) Some family or person in jealousy of the properties of the bride accepted Yoang-inba.Such a person (Yaong inba nupa) are looked down upon in the present society.

REFERENCES

1. Collonel Mecullock. The valley of Manipur. p. 19
2. M. Chandra singh- Panthoibi Khongul-P.35
3. Ibid.
4. Heirem Puwari Unpublished. Ms, p.3.
5. M. Gourachandra- Thawanthaba Hiran, p.9.
6. Kh. Chandrasekhar Loiyumba Shilyen, p.61.
7. T.C. Hudson. The Meithies, p.91.
8. Th. Madhop & N.Khelchandra.- Khunung leichat shajat, p.69.
9. M. Narendra- Koubarol Khungum(Koubrulol), p. 12.
10. N. Khelchandra Nugpal Pombi luwaoba, p. 19.

CHAPTER FOUR

THE CULTS OF DEAD & FUNERARY RITUALS IN THE TRADITIONAL MEITEI SOCIETY

Historical background of the disposal of the dead.

It is generally believed that, the present system of disposal of the dead of the Meitei owed its origin from the 18th century AD with the introduction of Hinduism in the state.But actually it is heritage of the past . From a careful study of their past history and culture there were two practices viz burial and cremation. A section of the people performed crematory method from time immorial which is very much similar to the customs of the Boro-Cacharis. The Chakpa-tribe who now formed scheduled caste in Manipur also performed cremation in their disposal of the dead. Their disposal of the dead is prototype of the Pyu of Burma who lived together with them for more than five centuries before Christian era in upper Burma.

According to Meitei chronicles, there were different forms of disposal of the dead practised in different political eras.

The history of the Meiteis most probably started by about 3rd century BC. It is devided into four eras viz 1) Hayichak 2) Haya chak 3) Khunung Lang bachak and 4) Kanachak as stated above. But their chronicles mentioned another four eras which is known as the era of Hangko i.e. 1) Ka - hangka 2) Thoi hangko 3) Ta/tayo hanko and 4) Poi hangko. But these eras are not related with the Meiteis. It is a period of proto history of the land before the advent of the Meiteis.

Their chronicles mentioned existence of four types of disposal of the dead, i.e. disposal in the air (Nungsitki potloi),disposal in the water (ishingi potloi),burial (Leipaki potloi) and cremation(Meigi potloi).

Further it is mentioned that, they performed different forms of disposal of the dead in different periods (eras). But those chronicles are not unanimous. In the first era of Hayichak, the disposal was in the water. But another chronicle Sakok lamen pointed out that, people of those days performed both the system of disposal in the air and water simultaneously. The dead body was kept for few days in the open field and then it was thrown in the water. The chakpa tribe was the ruler of the land at the beginning of the Hayi-chak. They performed cremation as disposal of the dead. The ashes and remains of bones were kept in an earthern pot and it was thrown in water or buried like the Pyu.The recent archaeological finding at Andro an important village of Chakpa testifies it. In the second era i.e Haya chak there were marked changes in the disposal of the dead and elaborate death ritual began to be performed. Probably it was due to the influence of religious preachers from East Bengal from the fact that, the role of purohit and singers were played by Urok and Usha respectively who came from Bengal. In the third era i.e Langha chak we find two distinct systems i.e burial and cremation side by side by different groups. The then system of cremation is very much akin to Boro Cachari.

There is a controversial point of views about the mode of disposal of the dead for the last era i.e Kon na chak. Chronicles like Sakok lamlen refer to cremation while chronicles like Thirel layat, Poireiton Khunthok and Ningchit give the account for the burial of the dead body. But it is quite clear that from the time of king Naothingkhong (8th century AD) burial system was prevalent in the Meitei society. A uniform system was introduced in the country after its completion of state formation in the 15th century AD. The system continued till 18th century AD before the introduction of Hinduism in the state. The present system of cremation came into existence with the coming of Hinduism. Though the rite and ritual are substituted by Hindu rite and ritual the process is in toto of the past.

Causes of Illness and Death

Manipuri (Meitei) terms of death are 1) Siba, 2) Lanba, 3) Lai- oikhiba, 4) Khamnung sawa tanba, 5) Aman-shingkumba, 6) Yamoi, 7) Nungsikhiba, 8) Korou-nongda kaba etc. But in general the term siba is commonly used.

According to the Meitei beliefs, there are many causes of one's death and illness.

1. Death after one's days are numbered. Death is due to the law of nature.
2. Death after being possessed by evil spirits who causes incurable illness. According to the general belief most ailments and diseases are brought about by the evil spirits. So to appease and exorsise the evil spirits, rituals are performed by priests and priestesses.

3. Death due to black art or witch craft:- In the early Meitei society tendency to make a person ill, short lived,blind,insane and dead by means of black magic as a result of jealousy or illfeeling due to a quarrel. There was a strong propensity to acquire mastery over black arts. So, the early Meiteis used to take precautionary measures to ward off black arts. The present practice of wearing amulets may be a continuation of this belief in witch craft (potsem waisem). Now and then the preist (Maiba) and priestess (Maibi) who practised black arts were beaten, punished and chastised by their kith and kin and neighbourers. In case the reports of black arts reached the king's ears, the persons envolved were duly punished. If the illness caused by black art was detected and treated in time, the victims might be saved from the jaws of death.

4. Death due to gradual weakening of the body as the result of an injury or accident which impaired and damaged the soul and spirit.

   It is believed that if a person is scared and frightened on account of injuries, beating by other people, fright, falling from tree, drowning etc, then his soul and spirit become void and impaired. In another word, some of the five elements of the soul leave the physical body of the patient or victim. As a result of these accidents and incidents, the victim becomes insane, mentally disordered, psychologically imbalanced, physically weakened and ultimately loses longevity. In these circumstances, if the soul shadow of the patient is called back in time, he may come round as before. The practice of calling back of the soul- shadow or spirit has been in vogue in

Meitei society since time immemorial if and when a man happens to fall ill or lose consciousness.

5) Repetition of premature deaths after births and miscarriage,ie. spontaneous expulsion of the foetus from the womb before it is able to live independently is believed to be perpetrated by an unclean spirit called Soren (poltergeist).

   To ward off and cure these evil symptoms, the Soren is appeased with a ritual prayer. For the welfare of the king and the kingdom a ritual ceremony called 'Hongnemba' is performed.

6) Death of women during child birth, death from drowning and outbreak of epidemic diseases like small pox and diahorrea are believed to be caused by evil spirits.

   Examining the above phenomena we may assume that untimely death was believed to be caused by demons or evil spirits, witch craft and emptiness of soul spirit.

7) In addition to natural death due to completion of one's life span, there is another manifestation of death which is the result of unprepardness and neglect at the critical conjunction of man's life (Langpham). Therefore, when there is critical conjunction in a man's life, a ritual sacrifice is performed as substitute for the victim (Ushin-sinba).

8) Unnatural, ugly deaths etc are considered to be the dispensation of justice by God.

9) There is one reason attributed to untimely death. The soul manifests in this mortal world for a brief while to carry out god's commands towards ultimate deliverance.

Life is not a bed of roses, foolish persons live by eating, drinking, and making merry till death. This world is not finite and constant. As the sunsets every day, the moon rises, days turn into months and months turn to years. In this way time itself comes to an end. Similarly, as the vital force of a man's life driwndles gradually day by day, it returns no more. The whetstone also dwindles bit by bit if regularly used to sharpen the knives. The knife, if used daily regularly, gradually diminishes and loses sharpness and strength in the long run. Likewise a man's life and energy also decays. Life can't be renewed as the snake casts off its slough.

At old age, when one's days are numbered, the senile man and woman are unable to execute their plans and dreams into action. Rather their plans and schemes misfire and retreat backwards. The spinal column becomes curved, masticating teeth age and dwindle, footsteps tend to be awry, the cheekbone becomes prominent owing to shrinkage, eyelids wrinkle and shrivel, the eye socket becomes shrunken deep, eyesight fails to recognize people and objects, the tips of fingers and toe become insensitive and numb, the wrist cannot turn freely and strumbling and tripping becomes a routine matter in every step. Finally, as the vital force of life diminishes by and by the end of existence becomes invitiable. So, man has utterly failed to carry out his intents and purposes to the fullest during his life time. When a man's life span, which is ordained by God, near completion this dear mortal body groans in extreme pain. Then enroute a vaccum in the spine, the wind blows up increasingly from each and every nook and corner of the body. The beating of pulses increases in intensity, the heat of the fire flame burns hotter and hotter water overwhelms all over the umbilicus, the physical body decays little by little on account of the gradual loosening of the spinal cord.

And when the time comes for the body and the soul to bid goodbye to each other, the heart lotus starts decaying. All the pulses begin to beat with unbearable heat and thirst for water overwhelms the dying men.

At the time the dying man will crave mita-khamta-chak a desire to eat something (rice).[1] As the wind blows up inside the mortal body the whole nervous system becomes stiff. And when the arteries have become inert all the latches, bolts and locks shutting the nine doors cavities (thonglon mapal) of the human body are withdrawn.

When the tying knot of the three fold body is undone, a tempestuous wind blows with overwhelming intensity throughout the body as if to overblow the lotus petals. As the blows through the noses upwards the stomach pit, the breast heaves upwards like a fluttering flag. As the ear drums are overwhelmed as if blocked, the power of hearing is lost. Then as the strong wind blow in one by one upto the sanaching, the ultimate stage, the lotus like eyes have fallen into the trap of the ordaining God to nobody's knowledge. As the overwhelming force of the wind increases, the immortal soul along with its shadow ray leaps out of the mortal body in the form of a ray.[2]

The crumbling of mortal body and departure of the soul from human body.

It is quite natural for the soul to leave the body after the life comes to an end owing to the gradual decaying of the mortal body as the result of an imbalance in fire, water and air due to the exhaustion of life-gem, the binding vital force of life. According to the Meitei belief, all this changing process and departure of the soul from the mortal body are the consequence of the attainment of the abode of God by guardian spirits or gods of the mortal body after leaving each and every limb. The mortal body is depicted as the abode of God. In each limb of the body dwells a God or a spirit. By virtue of holding and guarding the life gems which bind the vital force of life, all these Gods bring about motion and human birth. When they mis-step, causing thereby imbalance, there comes a change in the human body. It is believed that when the spirits have left the mortal body, life that existed in it have ceased. It is beyond possibility to discuss in detail in this book the abode of these Gods and also the places over which they stand watch and ward. The puya called "Singdabung kyan" exhaustively deals with these matters. Khamoi-yamoi, pombi-lang etc also treat with the above matters here and there only briefly. According to this belief, the vital force of the human body and its movement is under the guardianship and control of some spirits and the mortal body becomes inactive with their departure.

AFTER WORLD

Where the soul goes and dwells after departing the body.

It is believed that when critically ill or at the dying moment, the soul after departing the mortal body roams about; out of the five souls four souls go out while the fifth one called "Waba-apishak" stays behind unable to leave the body because of being bound by the knot of love for the near and dear ones. When the elemental force of external wind overwhelms, the whole five souls if ever left the body- it is considered to be the attainment of deliverance. Taking advantages of this juncture of the soul's exit, the female spirit of death called Khamnung-Kikoi-Louonbi-Nura-Poathem-Heibi leads the soul away from the body by means of persuasion and flattery. Impersonating as a parent or friend or beloved consort, the said female spirit of death makes the departing souls eat a peculiar beautiful fruit and smell a beautiful flower which disallows the soul to return to the body. Thus luring the soul by flattery upto the top of the Lalangpung mount, she feeds the soul with a mixture of ingredients called Wandengkhoibi Singju. Then the Goddess reveals her true identity and leaves the soul alone. Now the departed soul will cry and lament since he no longer can see the human world and find the entrance to the previous life., Then, after going some distance, the soul will skirt Tarung Goddess by the right side and go on the journey till it reaches the abode of Langol Ningthou. A little further it will reach the courtyard of Thongak Lairembi. It rests for a while after drinking water from the waterpot of the Goddess, kept especially for the departed souls. Then leaving Thongkhak Lairembi, it arrives at Khonghampat by and by. There the soul washes and cleans its feets and then washes cloth at Phisurok. Coming further, it takes out the fruits at Heirurok and then at Chayomlok unwraps the food packet to eat the meal. After that, it takes bath and rinses the head and hair with unboiled lye water .At the sight of human cross-road, the mind became romantically agitated, hence the place was called Makoi-nungonching. Seeing its dead body consigned to burning flame, or buried underneath the ground, it was again agitated and troubled. Then after reaching the sacred abode of Thongaren the soul crosses the river where the bridge is just one strand of hair and railing also of one strand of hair. Finally, it touches the feet of Thongaren's throne.

Opening the pages of the Anji Laiyum (Doomsday Book) Pishatao metes out justice according to the deeds done in the previous mortal world leading the virtous ones to the abode of the supreme God in heaven and throwing down the evil doers into the eighty four pits of hell. Another belief is for the pious man who staunchly believes in God, the god he worships will come to him at the last moment of death and carry him to God's abode. So, he does not face the trouble of the journey.

The above points indicate that alter death the soul goes to the abode of Thongaren, the God of death through a journey. Thongaren dispenses justice by examining the deeds the souls'did before their death and send either to heaven or hell. But according to another book "Garbha-Bichar" the destinations of the soul after death are given as under 1) death in heaven i.e accession to heaven, 2) entry into womb i.e. rebirth. 3) Death on the earth (born in inferior position as plant, insect etc.) and 4) death in nether i.e. going to hell. Thus souls are destined to different destinations according to their deeds.

Unlike the Hindu concept of Narak in which the evil doers are punished with great tortures in hell, Meiteis believe that to fall into hell is nothing but living a sorrowful and pitiable life while living in the actual world and not in the next life. So, there is a far wide difference in the concept of hell between the Meiteis and the Hindus. But its basis or framework is borrowed from the Hindu.

Where the soul dwells before being born in the mortal world ?

The soul who ascends to heaven will attain salvation by being absorbed into the Supreme One.

Some blessed souls, before getting the salvation live with their ancestors in the heaven. They are either born on this earth or get deliverance by uniting with the Almighty God. But there arises a question, where the other souls that will be reborn in the mortal world, dwell before rebirth.

One opinion is such souls transform into rice, curry, vegetables, grasses,weeds,flowers and fruits for a temporary period and then are reborn in the mortal world.[3] Another opinion is before being reborn these souls exist in different places in different matters i.e five days in the earth, five days in invertebrate insects, five days in legless animals, sixteen days in the sun, eight days in the sky and five days in the star.[4] That means there is a gap of time, 44 days before being reborn in the human world.

Though there is some difference of the objects they exist in before being reborn, it is quite clear that, the souls exist in certain objects and there is a gap of time before being reborn in a human life. For the souls of the common people it is generally believed that a soul may be reborn after the completion of all the death rituals ie after one year. But for virtuous persons or blessed souls they may be reborn at any time under the blessing of the Almighty God or get salvation. For them no elaborate rituals are required.

The souls that are unable to get deliverance cannot dwell either in heaven or in earth and therefore remain hovering at the place of their death or in the sky. Such souls haunt, disturb and frighten their former family members and whomever they meet and even cause illness and unhappiness to them. Therefore to deliver these undelivered souls or to prevent them from interfering with man many rituals are performed, say a) shutting the gate of death (mang thong thingba) b) offering oblation to appease the souls for no reoccurrence of unwanted things and for no reappearance of their selves (Chupsha-moithemba) c) feasting the dead (Asi- Aman-Chak-Khangba) and d) obstruction of Soren.

Another opinion is the souls that have departed their mortal bodies live with their ancestors in the heaven. Therefore, at the time of Phunga-apokpa worship, Moon and Polestar are prayed to for sending invitation to the forefathers dwelling in heaven. At the time of begging boons and blessings, it is believed that the great grand father only has the power to grant boons. Great grandfather passes the boon and blessings to the grandfather who in turn passes it to father who finally passes it to the prayer. So, the great grandfather enjoys the status of a God who can bless and endow boons.[5] Again, in all life circle ceremonies of the traditional Meitei society the spirits of the ancestors (pu'rol-Ahum) are summoned and begged for their blessings. So, such believes of the Meiteis are very much akin to Hindu concept of Pitrilok.

Another belief is, if my grandson begot by my son (ishu) offers something to God on his grand grand father's behalf the soul representing the great grand father will be enhanced to the status of a god. Untill and unless he gets that status he will be in the status of demi-God. The god turned souls will now be in the assembly of Gods in the heaven.So goes a Meitei adage,for the deliverance of the soul it is the son and for riding the flower palanquin it is the grandson.[6]

Concept of Heaven

Like the Hindu concept of Swarga and Naraka the Meiteis also believed in the existence of Korou-nongthou Leibak and Khamnung warak. We cannot say for sure if this belief is an influence of the Hindu philosophy or if it originally belonged to the Meitei element of thought. Some people may unthinkingly assert it as the influence of Hindu philosophy. But the concept of Heaven and Hell and belief in them have been existing since time immemorial among the people of Chin hills, Tibet and South east Asia. The Riangs , one of the tribes in north east India have a similar concept like the Meiteis. Therefore it warrants an indepth study to ascertain which concept influenced the Meiteis.

The Meities describe Heaven in different names like Korou-nongthou Leibak, Nungnang Kao khangkol, Konkhei-Atamba etc. The chief objective of the Meitei religion is a man should be virtuous so that after death his soul will ascend to Korou nongthou (Heaven) and attain the divine status to unite with the Supreme one. According to this religious belief evil men by virtue of their deeds are reborn to a more lowly state. This process of being reborn to lower and lower strata will continue till ultimately their souls vanish to nothing or may improve themselves and be reborn in a better status. The Meitei view is there is no place called Hell. The souls of evil-minded- lowly men are reborn to the state of fish, insect, reed or to a wretched, pitiable and impoverished condition of a deseased, disfigured and ill-starred man. Such sorry state of things is called Khamnung warak i.e. punishment in hell.[7] Therefore, the Meitei concept of hell is quite different from the Hindu concept.

Where lies Korou-nongthou Leibak or Heaven?

It is worth asking where lies the Korounongthou Leibak where the Gods dwell and the departed souls of virtous men reach after death. There are three places under the Meitei belief where the Gods dwell. They are—a) Koubru hill, b) Seloi-langmai hill (Nongmai-ching) and c) Thangching hill. It is clearly mentioned in Takhangba- Nongaron' that five successive kings of Ningthouja clan from Nongda-lairen Pakhangba to Noaphangba made ascension to heaven in flesh and blood. The Tibetans too have a similar belief like the Meitei account.However the book does not mention the routes and places undertaken by these Kings. But the journey of Chothethangwai Pakhangba and Leima Shunulembi to Korou-nongthou leibak is given at the behest of sky God Soraren. The names of the Korou-nongthou leibak in the text are given as 1) Korou-nonglangpan, 2)

Nungnang-Kaokhamkon, and 3) Kongkhei atamba. If we study comparatively the places given in the mythological account of earth creation (Leishemba), the place called Kongkhei atamba was the abode of the Atiya Kuru Sidaba. The place is referred to as Tarang Ching. In the early days Seloilangmei Ching was known as Tarang ching or Sanaching and from Langmaiching the name Nongmai ching was derived.

The history of settlement according to Meitei creation mythology was started from the present Chingkhei hill. The hill was known by different names in those days viz, Kurum ching, Tarang- ching, Kanglei nungnangphan etc. There lies the abode of konkhei-Atamba and that of the Soraren. It was at Konkhei-Atamba that Atiya-Kuru-sidaba made his abode. So, the place itself is described as the top of the heaven. The above view is supported by Singtabung kyan an unpubllished manuscript. “It is Leimaren whom air encircles”. “It is Atiya sidaba whom the water encircles”. Both are called Nongthou Mayon (top of the heaven). The one who can trace the top is known as one who can climb nongthou (heaven). It indirectly infers that, the abode of Atiya sidaba and Leimarel sidabi is the heaven.

Concept of the Soul

According to the Meitei belief there are five souls. And it is accompanied by a shadow. So, it has often been customary to chant five souls and a shadow (Thawai-manga-miga-thana-taruk). That means the human body is composed of six things including five souls and a shadow.

These five souls are generated by the aura of the supreme God. The name of the five souls are respectively 1) Tinan 2) Neno, 3) Tatan, 4) Piyan and 5) Yapi. It is believed that each soul has a custodian god. They are :- 1) Nongthanglen (

Koubru)dwelling in the cerebrum 2) Apanba dwelling in the umbilias 3) Thangjing dwelling in the pelvis below navel, 4) Marjing in the heart and 5) Wangbaren who dwells in the urethra. Thus the five souls dwell in different parts of the human body.[8] They sometimes change their position in the human body in a diurnal period. This is called soul becoming void and impairment of the shadow spirit. Sometimes some of those five souls may go out of the body. This is also called soul becoming void and impairment of the shadow- spirit. (Thawai-hamchatnaba-miren-hampoinaba). If a part of the body frequently throbs, then it is believed that, the soul spirit has taken its seat there. But scientifically it is not true.

Origin and Nature of Soul

It is generally believed the soul is an image of the Supreme God. To be born in human life the soul emanates from the Supreme God and passing through different natural phenomena one by one, enters the maternal womb. The lord of universe (Taibangpanba-gi-mapu) passes the soul to the sun, the sun to the Moon, the moon to the Evening star,the evening star to the Morning star,the Morning star to the Okpuroi, Okpuroi to Taohuireng,Taohuireng to father, Father carries it for two months and passes it to the mother and finally mother conceives it for ten months in the womb.[9]

Their chronicles also classified the soul into four types according to their quality. But its exact meaning is not yet ascertained. They are 1) soul born of the belly, 2) soul born unconceived. 3) soul going breathwise and 4) soul going length wise.[10] The quality of soul is different from one person to another in accordance with the deeds done by individuals during mortal life both past and present. The soul of a virtous individual is said to be a perfect soul.

The perfect soul of a such person attain the deliverance or salvation after death. The souls of evil men will gradually decline step by step by being reborn to the lower status of the beast,fish,insect etc etc ultimately they will dwindle into a void. Hence Meitei concept is quite opposed to the immortality of soul.

After departing the bodies.the soul transform into different versions - soul at the status of a God, soul that has attained the statue of a demi-God,soul that has changed into the shape of a demon or devil. The souls of the forbears are believed to make visitations upon their descendents and get involved in the joys and sorrows of their family members. To obtain, their blessings , the Meiteis perform ancestor worship (family ancestors, phunga apokpa, ancestor of the sub clan, Sagei apokpa and that of the clan.Salai-apokpa). Those souls who could not get the deliverance indulge in disruptive and destructive activities.

It will be very wonderful to know that, majority of the Gods the Meitei worship take the role of a demon or devil and tend to indulge in obstruction and destruction. If a person comes across with such spirits or if they are not gratified or propitiated, the person is sure to suffer from destruction, ruin, illness or ill health. Even Sanamahi whom the Meiteis worship with reverence and awe sometimes takes the role of a devil (Apoiba). We find such forms of deities among the tribes.

The lord of the universe causes rebirth of the souls in human forms for a particular mission. The soul that has achieved the assignment or mission will again enter into him. Those who fail in their mission will be reborn again and again. At last the defeated souls will not be able to reborn in human form, but in a meaner manifestation as stated above. So, the Meitei Maichous (scholars) made the remark that: -"Man dies to be reborn and vice-versa".

In these souls are still present the six vices, namely, jealousy, envy, desire, anger, sorrow and love. To be brief, those who are in the snares of worldly matters will be reborn again and again in mortal bodies. As long as these weaknesses cannot be abandoned, the soul can never get deliverence or salvation.[12] A unique feature of the Meitei philosophy is besides a stage when the soul becomes weakened and inert, it may also go out of the human body and strays about. This is called the impaiurment and voidness of the soul-spirit. The causes of this situation are- 1) becoming physically weak,2) scare or fright due to faling from the tree, drowning in water etc. 3) lying critically ill, 4) Living under the captivity of the demons or evil spirits, 5) the soul-spirit being called away, captived and ruined by sorcery or witchcraft.

If the soul continues to remain outside its physical body for a considerable length of time the person to whom belongs the soul becomes mentally deranged without being dead at all. This is what the Hindus call Brahma-bhrama. Then the person becomes insane and mad. It is also believed that even while a man is alive his soul goes outside a while. If we dream that we are wandering in distant places, are at a loss to return home and wake up before reaching our home, it is believed to be symptom of our soul staying abroad. The Meitei maibas (Priest cum physicians) can diagnose this symptom by feeling the pulse of the afflicted person. This Meitei belief of the souls' temporary sojourn outside the body is also prevalent among the Kuki tribes, particularly the Paite tribes.

Means for remedy

Different practices were performed by the Meiteis to cure the impairment and voidness of the soul spirit. 'Mikon-thakonba' a ritual of embracing the soul-spirit was one of such type used to be performed in the villages on the last day of the Lai- Haroaba festival. But this practice is no longer prevalent. For the souls of those scared of their wits due to fright, the amaiba or amaibi (female priestess) used to perform the ritual of soul calling (Thawai-mi- Koushinba). But in general when small children fall in water and fall from the bed etc, the parent calls back the soul-spirit of the child and puts it into the concerned child's mouth. It was generally believed that, the soul- spirit left the body of the child if frightened. The Meiteis believed that when a man comes across demons or evil spirits or when they are not appeased or propitiated, they keep the soul and body of the man in their clutches and cause illness, derangement and madness to them. Before the advent of the modern science most causes of illness were attributed to the demons and evil spirits. A probable reason why the tribals of Manipur embraced Christainity was belief in, Christ could save them from oppression by demons.

It was a frequent phenomenon that many people who were possessed by witches, female spirits, nymphs and ghosts suffered from derangement and insanity. We have seen its trace till now. In such circumstances the amaiba or amaibi exorcises the haunting spirit or demons either by force or by propitiation.

In early days there was tendency among the 'Meiteis to ruin a person by means of black art (magic) owing to jealousy, envy or enmity. In this regard the Meiteis were highly proficient. Not only this, there were many forms of black arts. If one woman would like to make a man her own, black arts were employed. Women tried to keep their husbands under their thumb by using black magic or destroy the health of their rivals. The main features we find in the latter case were calling out the soul of the person to keep it under captivity, lure, weaken and render it unable to go back to the former self.Love charms of different forms like- Tareng leibi, Mikourol etc. are such arts. However, we rarely see the total annihilation of the soul. For the soul which was supposed to have been destroyed or under captivity could be recreated and called back to its former self with the help of masters (MaibaX Maibi) adept in this field.

When one is critically ill, his soul goes out of the body for a brief period and wanders about. So, a special ritual ought to be performed for calling back the departed soul-spirit.

A unique feature of the Meitei concept of soul is man can talk with his own soul by calling it out of his body. It is believed that expert in magic and witchcraft can talk and ask to his own soul everything he wants to know by calling it out by incanting magic (tantra) words of potency. This deed is usually carried out at the dead of midnight when no sound and voices would be heard. This art of talking with the soul is known as Brahma- Sanaba (playing with the Brahma).

Almost similar with the above Brahma-playing, there is another method of knowing the secret information known as Mingshen-Kanglon (crystal grazing). Under this method, one can know everything one wants to know in dream by be searching the soul with rites. Not only the information wanted, the soul communicates to the concerned person the future events as well as the events connected with his friends and relatives. Another practice of the same type called Mangdaba (Seance) was also prevalent among the Meiteis.

When the soul becomes void or during illness and sickness, the goddess of death, Khamnung Sidanubi alia Khamnung Kikoi Louonbi by impersonating different forms wheedles and tricks the person to whom belongs the soul to go the land of death. A detailed treatment has already been given earlier. It is therefore, advised that one should not succumb to her flattery and coaxing or else one will suffer untold miseries after death. From the above point of view we can conclude that the soul is an entity which has divine power or divine manifestation and roams within and outside the human body.

The Theory of Rebirth

A strong belief of the Meiteis is "If born, will die, if dead will be born and vice versa". Like the Hindus, the Meiteis also firmly believe in the theory of rebirth. The lord of the universe emits from his divine self a divine ray to represent the soul and sends it to the human life on a special mission. It has already be mentioned earlier that the soul which has failed in this mission will be reborn again and again in the human world. As in Buddhism, to get released from the wheel of life and death the soul should attain the status of a perfect soul and then enter into God himself. People who have not yet attained this perfect stage suffer continuous rebirth.

The main objective of the Meitei religion is devotion to God and salvation after death by being a virtuous man during the lifetime. There are broadly two ways of deliverance (salvation) of soul. First the soul enters into god and thus gets freedom from the wheel of life and death. Second, to be born again in human life. If I undergo rebirth at the moment I die, this is freedom or deliverance of soul.Though there are some similarities with Hindu and Buddhist concepts, the latter concept of deliverence or salvation in Meitei religion is utterly different. Until the soul attains the status of a god after becoming a perfect soul, it undergoes rebirth times out of number.

In the death ritual also a ceremony called Chak-Khang thou (feasting celebration) is held to feast the members of the Sagei (sub clan), specially the women members , and a ritual prayer is made so that the soul of the dead man may undergo rebirth by entering the womb of a good woman.[13] Now, after the advent of Hinduism this Chakkhang thou ceremony is replaced by a function called 'Divas' which is held on the next day of the shardha ceremony (death ceremony) by way of tasting fish which was restricted to the family. In this ceremony of Divas alias Ngatangba all the participants in the cremation of the dead body are entertained with a grand feast. Accordingly the original underlying ideas are no longer understood as a new different trend has developed.

When selecting daughters-in-law, parents would essentially select ideal and virtuous maidens in the hope that they would be their mothers in the next birth. A strong belief in this regard is the birth of a new child is the return of their departed elders or their recently deceased children. Some bereaved parents who believed in this belief lament the demise of the beloved child in such a way that it be reborn to them. Under the belief they put identifying marks (smearing) on the dead body of their child as we find among the Bodos and Riangs. Those identifying marks will be found in the opposite direction in the next life of the child. Another belief is the souls of unlucky and ugly deaths incarnate in the forms of animal, insect and tree and not in human form. For an instance, when Haoshi Namoinu was hit on the head with a ladle by her step mother her soul transformed into a Cicada.[14] Rebirth in human form or other object depends much upon the nature of one's death.

The Concept of Mukti or Salvation

Diliverence of soul from the mortal body after death is known as 'Lana-Khubam-phangba'. To reach the abode of god by the departed soul is the main theme of the traditional Meitei religion. So, in the death ceremonies elaborate rituals (Lana thouram) were performed. Those souls who could not reach the abode of the God become unclean spirits. According to Meitei philosophy Salvation or Mukti is of three types. First, the soul leaves the mortal body and remerges with god. This concept is hardly different from the Hindu concept of Sayurya-mukti and Nirvana of Buddhism. Second, rebirth in human form after death is also called Salvation by the Meiteis. But all the rebirth are not be treated as if who get Salvation only those form through the blessings of Almighty God be regarded as Apokpa-lanba (deliverance by birth). This type of salvation is of two forms. Third, people exalt those men who established the immortal tree of eternal fame to the status of gods and worship them with adortion. This form of Salvation is very similar to the Surupa mukti of the Hindus.

How The Soul Got Deliverence or Salvation

Merging with the Almighty God by the soul after release from the wheel of birth and death is known as Salvation (Lana-khubam-phangba) by the Meiteis. This form of Salvation is the ultimate and absolute one. This is very similar to Sayurja of the Hindus and Nirvana of the Buddhists as stated above. How can salvation be attained. The wisemen who have conquered jealousy, envy, desire, enmity, anger, sorrow and love by cherising god in their hearts are called perfect souls. (Mee-Maru-Mee-Maahen) that have attained the status of a god. The soul of such a man merges with god after departing from the mortal body. To reach this stage there are seven paths viz, 1) Calmness of mind 2) Virtue, 3) right speech, 4) right spirit 5) protection to life, 6) steadfastness 7) memory of God. The soul that can observe these principles will get deliverance. One who has conquered the five senses, eye, ear, nose, tongue and mind will no more tread the path of sins.[15] This concept must have been in all probality an influence of Buddhism.

Another concept of the deliverance of the soul is rebirth in human form. Rebirth in human form after entering into the womb of Guru (Almighty God) is said to be salvation. But rebirth in other forms do not attain salvation. Now rebirth though the womb of Guru is of two ways: -1) Rebirth in the human life by resigning oneself to God before death and 2) rebirth in human form by resigning oneself to God after death through ancestors.

Death is inevitable someday. Wisemen, therefore, chart out the future course of action after death during their lifetime. Like the leech spanning from one tip of grass to another tip of grass, man also during lifetime should plot his plan to heaven in order to merge with God after death. Then only, God will accept the attitude and conduct of the man himself and say' Come to me, be born as my child'. If I am born again on the very day I die this is also verily salvation. This is known as salvation through the womb (Garbhada-Changbs-lanba). If a child is ever born in the family or to nearest relative on the very day of one's death his soul enters the child.[16]

Another form of salvation is entry into the belly of the grandfather through the medium of the father. The grandfather brought the soul to the Almighty God (Guru) and if ever blessed allowed the soul for rebirth in human form. When grandfather has shown the seed of generation rebirth in human form happens. This type of deliverance of soul is known as salvation through ancestor. It is indirect form of Garbha-da-changba-lanba.[1?]

The above two forms of salvation differ only in form and time. They are all rebirths in human form.The first is rebirth on the very day of death and the second is rebirth via father after the soul has left the body and stayed with the ancestors for sometime waiting the blessing of the Almighty God. Such type of deliverance is rarely seen in other religions. This is a distinct concept of the Meiteis. But for this uniquely distinct form or concept the Meitei religion might have been considered an offshoot of Hinduism or Buddhism.

An important point worthy of discussion about salvation is the Meitei exalted men and women of extraordinary distinction (cultural hero and heroine and political heroes) to the status of god and worshipped them. Men who had established immortal tree of eternal fame are exalted as god or goddess with reverence and awe. For an instance Imoinu Ahongbi, Phouoibi-Lairembi etc. Because Imoinu Ahongbi appeared with Atiya-Sidaba in abundance and prosperity she has been worshipped as the goddess of wealth. Likewise, when all the other goddesses had failed to produce paddy in abundance Phouoibi-Lairembi produced it in abundance and hence she has also been worshipped as the goddess of paddy. It is worth questioning whether such people as had established eternal fame had attained salvation since the souls of such people were exalted to the status of gods or goddesses. Likewise political heroes like Khagemba, Naothingkhong etc are also worshipped as gods who earned undying fame by their achievement. In the same way, heroes and pratiots, who have laid down lives without ever tuning their backs in the battlefield are supposed to have ascended to heaven directly.

Preparation for the Disposal of the Dead

The Meiteis considered the dying moment of a man to be very serious and loked after him carefully and attentively. For the soul to go in the right path to merge with God, so preparations including ritual performance were made with the help of scholars and knowledgeable persons. A maiba was engaged to watch and attend to the dying man. In the early days, there was a vogue that members of the local death organisation called Shinglup stood watch by lighting fire (Mei-lingba) at the residence of the dying man in turn. By feeling the pulse of the dying man the maiba could presage the day and hour of the death of the dying person. However, since the symptoms of illness of different persons were different, great wakefulness and watchfulness was required for the dying person. Articles and materials required for funerary function were arranged before hand. According to the instruction of the maiba, Yathokshang (a make shift shed in the courtyard) was made. But for those who bury their dead, as the dead body was required to be kept inside the house for five days, Yathokshang was not to be set up early. Now a day the dead person is carried over to Yathokshang before the person breathes his last or while there is still some vestige of Brahma in his body. With the advent of Hinduism those who are to be ordained to 'Sanyas' should be ordained so while there is still respiration in the dying body. That is why the Meiteis take great pains to watch the dying moment of a person without fail, when the dying man begins to breath by moving his chin, then he is brought to the 'Lapyan-Ka' (the front room of the typical Meitei house) where the person is laid on a white cloth over a mat for sometime.But due to Hindunised influence this is done in the porch of the house. While the dead body is lying in the Layan-Ka for five days, all his relatives and friends and acquaintances visit him for the last time and condole his death. During these five days, those who visited the deadman are entertained with food and drinks. For those who cremate their dead body it was not necessary to lay the dead body for five days. It was cremated on the same day. But if it was happened during the night, the dead body was kept for the whole night.

While the dying man is still breathing, so as to enable him to go on the right path and to let him not fall into hell, the maiba will perform ritual of shutting and opening the door. The door here means the path in which soul has left the mortal body. The door is opened through the navel, the centre of the eye-brows and the crown of the head. Untill the dead body is carried to the Yathokchang the maiba will detain the vestige of Brahma (soul) of the dying man by placing his palm on the navel of the dying man.

The residents of the locality who belong to the Shinglup are informed of the death by beating drums and striking iron rods. The courtyard is cleared and Yathoksang is created at Khagenpham (south eastern part of the courtyard). A waterpot is laid on the ground and on it a flag is attatched in a slanting position. If the body is to be cremated, there is laid an earthen pot called Meikoi- chaphu and another pot which contains fire. Preparation for rites and rituals are made by depositing some paddy called Yangphou. Some chronicles mentioned the performance of ritual like the Pinda-Piba of the Hindus for the cremation community. A new route will be made by cutting down the fence on the east side of the residential compound and all the rear doors of the house should be closed.[18] But it generally believed that the burial of the dead body was made in the residential compound itself before King Naothingkong (8th century A.D) as he introduced the system of burial for each and every specific sub-clan (sagei) at a particular area. The courtyard is cleared and cleaned and then arrangement is made to feast the relatives of the family.

When all the relatives of the family have assembled and lamented, the dead body is carried to the Yathokshang (temporary hut for the corpse). The hair is washed with lyewater (chenghi), the body is bathed, the nails are cut and then is dressed with white clothes right to left. Then it is placed on a plaintain leaf in the Yathokshang with the head north wards on a headrest made of plaintain trunk or pillow made of shangbrei leaves. Then the body is wrapped by a mat of bamboo. Four sticks is planted along the navel, unspun cotton thread is wound three times round the sticks. The thread is raised upto the funeral ground. The ritual is called poromthopthinba. A coin is placed in the ear and a piece of iron bid on the back. Most of the important articles used by the person during his or her lifetime were put in the burial. Otherwise, it is generally believed that the spirit frequently disturbed the family for its demand. After the amaiba has performed the rituals in accordance with the customs, then the dead body is placed in a coffin which is carried over the shoulders by the children and relatives of the deceased on foot along with the beatings of drums and cymbals accompanied by a funeral song upto the funeral ground.lt is believed that, before King Naothingkhong (8th century) the burial took place inside the enkhol of the family like the local tribes. But how far it is true is a question of further investigation. In the early times funeral songs (yaithongnanam or Amansingkumsei) was sung by the elder women of the locality.[19] But with the advent of Hayachak era, the Usha from Bengal undertook the tasks of singing the funeral song.[20]

It has already been mentioned before that with the advent of the Langbachak era the disposal of the dead appeared in two forms, viz, burial and cremation. In the two forms, the funeral procedures and rituals were similar in many aspects. In both forms the practice of buying land for a grave was common. The Kachins had a custom of offering an animal or bird to mother goddess earth as a price for the grave. Butthe Meiteis performed this practice of buying land by offering anything they could afford, preferably wine. Now the land for the grave is bought by offering a coin.

Burial Process

The practice of burial for the disposal of the dead had begun since the second Chak called Hayachak. This practice continued until the Meiteis embraced Hinduism. During the long period of time there were several additions and alterations in this form. It would be difficult to definitely state how the various forms of burial were practised during the previous two eras of Hayachak and Langbachak eras.

Even in the Konachak, a marked change was perceptible in the burial form practised during the time of king Naothingkhong. (8th century AD). The forms of burial described in the Meitei Puya might be those practised in Konachak era.The form of burial process prevalent in those days might be compared with that of the white Miao or Meo in Southern Szechawn in China.[21] Therefore, it is absolutely necessary to have a detailed comparative study of the cultures and traditions of these two ethnic peoples.

The dead body is carried in a coffin to the family or clan burial ground and buried there in a space allotted for it according to age group. It is not known what rituals were performed at the time of burial, like the cremated group the expert (amaiba) prayed the Almighty God and decease ancestors of the dead person for the journey and permission to include in their abode. After buying the land, the coffin was placed and all the belongings of the person were also buried along with the body for its use in the journey and in land of the dead. Mangchak (a meal) will be offered and then the ritual of Mangthong Thingba (the path of the spirit to the mortal world be closed) was performed.

After one year when the new moon is over, the dead body is exhumed by chanting the rite of mangthong hangba (opening the gate of the grave).[22] Everything enclosing the corpse. (Porom) will be removed. The fleshy part is taken out to obtain the bone. The head is to be secured meticulously by wrenching it off the throat. The hair should be removed from the skull. All slimy substances and fluids are absorbed out. The brain (cerebrum) is cleaned out. The skull (cranium) and other bones are washed three times in a basket. After this they are left exposed to the sun for five days. Except the skull and other bones all the remains of the corpse are put in a basket called Shakuwalong and buried underground. When the skull is exposed in the sun for five days, facial part will discompose and fall apart. During exposure, a shed is erected over the skull. Bow, arrow and snare are hung around the shed to scare off the birds. So due care was taken to protect the skull. From the time of king Naothingkhong, allocation of duties for the above purposes was made to different subclans (sagei). At the sametime certain development can be witnessed in due course during the reign of later kings. Thus we find some differences in the procedure and ritual between the common people and the royal family. Then on an auspicious day, the skull and the bones will be buried again.

However the skull should be wrapped in a cloth and placed into a pot and covered by an earthern lid.[23] But in the case of a king and his family members, the skull is covered by a brass mask and embossed with gold or silver on the forehead. But it was done only by the select few.[24] The skull is brought in the grave once again accompanied by a party of singers and buried under due norms.Then a mound (mangpung) is raised by covering the burial ground with earth. The rituals of Mangchakthaba and Mangthong thingba are performed once again. The forms of burial, primary and secondary burial as described in the Meitei Puyas are closely testified by the recent archaeolocial findings. It is comparable with the culture of white Miao or Meo or Hung tribe of Southern Szechawn in China. Probably the culture was brought by Lai-Salai.

Crematory Process

From the dying moment to the laying of the corpse at the courtyard, all the ritual functions and. procedures observed by both the burial group and cremation group were similar in many aspects. But unlike the burial group, the corpse was not kept inside the house for five days. There were many points of differences in the matter of dress of the dead body, rite and rituals and its procedure.

A space is cleared for cremation and some fruit and pan is laid on the ground for buying the mangpham. Then seven layers of fuel logs including the ground layer will be laid. It means there must be only six layers of the logs. But among the Bodo-Kacharis, the number of layer differs according to sex. If the deceased person is a female there must be seven layers and another seven layers would be placed over the corpse. For a male, the layers must be only five in number in the same procedure as above.[25] Six posts will be erected round fuel logs. With four bamboo poles known as

'Uchiwa' is erected in the side of the fuel logs a little away and an awning called Chanduwa is raised high over the fuel logs as a canopy (thakan). A water pit is dug in the direction in which the head of the corpse may lie. Though there is a certain custom to place the corpse with the head northwards, if however, there is a tank or river or lake, its legs should not turn towards the water.

When the funeral pyre is fully prepared, the corpse placed in coffin is brought by the relatives and kins accompanied by a band of singers. The corpse is carried round the fuel logs. After the completion of three rounds the corpse is laid on the pyreThe bathing the cropse is done at the funeral ground instead at the residential compound of the dead. Offering fruits and flowers, kneading flour into a bal and offering it with black sesame, rice and dog grass (Tingthou), the Nongpal Amaiba (priest) invokes the ancestors of the departed soul and pray them so that they merge with the Supreme lord. Next, offering fruits and flowers by the water pit, the amaiba invokes fire god and worship the deity with ritual prayers. The fire for cremation is obtained from 'meiba' (primitive style for procuring fire) or from the hearth of the deseased family. It is brought in an earthern pot by burning paddy husk.

Then the man who will undertake the task of watching the funeral grave (mang-sangba), after taking a bath will carry a pot (meikoi-chaphu) full of water on the shoulder with a knife and a burning wood stump with the other hand (left hand). In this condition he will circle albng with all the family members and relatives, round the funeral pyre in the clockwise direction as the last oblation to deceased person. At the four corners water will be poured from the water pot and the burning wood stump will touch the fuel logs. This process will be done seven times for a female and five times for a male. But nowadays there is no distinction between male and female. Seven times is usually performed. This process is known as Mei-Koiba (Puroi-Leikoiba). After that the pyre is lit, the burning pyre is fanned with a fan made from the winnowing basket of the family till the corpse burns into ashes. On the eve of departing from the funeral, the man who will be taking up the task of watching the grave will offer to the burning pyre seven pieces of wood and each time he will strike the four poles of the pyre by an axe or a knife. Then by uprooting the four Uchiwa, the canopy (chandawa or Soinai pataruk) spanning high over the pyre is pulled over the burning body and made to burn itself. So that the Chandawa may fall exactly on the dead body, the fan may be employed. The four poles of Uciwa also are cut up into pieces.

The female participants in the funeral possession should also throw the pieces of wood into the burning pyre. At the time of leaving the funeral grave, they should take off the cloth wrapped around their heads and again wrap it round their waists. They will compete to reach a nearby tank or river first. After taking a bath the woman who first reached the bathing place will lead the grave leaving procession by singing mangka-eshei (grave leaving rite or song) At the gate of the deceased family they pass over a fire and are sanctified with toon leaves. (Tairel) by the husband of family's daughter. They are feed mangka singju (Manga= grave leaving, singju=salad).[26]

Meanwhile at the cremating ground, when all the body is brunt to ashes, the unbrunt remains of the bone are retrieved by means of tongs and put in a new earthen pot covered by an earthen lid and wrapped by a cloth or thread (Lang ahingba). The pot is then consigned to the water. After cleaning the funeral spot, a mound is raised, mangchak (oblation with rice) is offered and the ritual of mangthongthingba is done. The participants in the cremation will leave the funeral grave to take a bath in a nearby tank or river and go home. Passing over a fire, they are sanctified with toon leaves. Then thay fed on mangka-singju as before.

Changes During Kona Chak Era

The same form of cremation in the Langbachak was also prevalent in the Konachak era with certain alteration and addition here and there. For instancc, while the body is burning and reaching the stage of burning the head of the corpse some pieces of the burning body were cut for disposal by air, disposal by water and disposal by earth (ie a piece was thrown away in the open air, a piece was consigned to the water and a piece was buried). When the cremating of the dead was over, the grave was covered with earth to raise a small mound which was washed clearly with mud and water. Then the fruits and pan were offered to the deity presiding over the grave. In this way the gravemound would be entrusted to the spirit. Then by scattering some good seeds of mustard or seasame over the grave mound, the spirit of the departed would be persuaded to dwell there. On the grave a perch was made by fixing two sticks and a waterpot full to brim was suspended on it. Pricking a small hole at the bottom of the watepot, drops of water would be made to fall slowly on the grave. Then a hut or shed would be erected over it.

When all activities relating to the disposal of the dead were over, an elderly man would tread on stone, with a sword in hand and declare a solemn oath, “May this incident happen only once in this family in 100 years”. But now, with the advent of Hindunisation, though all the forms and traditions are observed without any change, the rites and rituals have been Hindunised. The solemn declaration of the oath also has been replaced by a cry of ganga-prapti.

Disposal of the dead bodies of those who died of an unnatural and abnormal death

Dead bodies of those who died of obnoxious diseases were buried if they belonged to the cremation group. But if the dead person belonged to the burial group, the dead body was cremated. If a man died with swollen belly due to meeting with a python, his corpse was placed on a raft or in a coffin which was made to float down the river along with an oil lamp in an earthen censer on the forehead. The same was the case with a dead of pregnant woman. For the latter case, the child in the womb had to be removed. In case the child was also dead, it was disposed of along with the mother.[27]

Children who died before three years of age were buried. Suicides were left in the wilderness. People who died from being burnt by fire,people died from drowning, falling from high places of tree, who got killed by other people or in the battle field, they were all disposed of according to their respective funeral ritual. For these types of death a ritual called "Chupsha- moithemba" was performed, people who died with punishment by royal order were also buried. Orphans and stranger found dead on the road were also buried. Such burials were performed by royal executioners.[28]

The philosophy behind the disposal of the dead

There was a philosophy of very high order among the people who disposed of the dead by cremation. A deep philosophy about the relation between man and nature and human soul was there. All activities related with the disposal of the dead seemed to have been performed with meaningful ideas.

The laying of seven layers of fuel logs for the cremation of the dead indicates that all men are born and die on one of the seven days of the week. The erection of six posts of bamboo round the pyre signifies that men if born in this world, would suffer according to natural phenomena, the influence of six seasons in a year, each season consisting of two months or would live under the influence of winter of six seasons and summer of six seasons. The three strands of thread or bamboo strips tying round the six posts indicates that human body is controlled by the three elements i.e fire, water and air. The planting of four bamboo poles for raising the Chanduwa implies that all the human beings exists within the four corners of the earth. The canopy above indicates the sky is above. And the layer of fuel log represented by ground means the earth is below. In short, mankind exists between the sky and the earth. To be brief, we human beings are under the influences of nature. The concept of the human body being constituted by fire, water, air, earth and ether expounds that we human beings are handiwork of nature.

When the soul departs the mortal body, it leaves for the abode of Thongaren, the god of death. It is believed that according to one's deeds in the previous world, the god of death ordains whether he or she will be ushered to the Supreme God or thrown into hell. For the use by the departed soul during his journey towards the abode of the god of death and in the land of god, it was in vogue to lay down coin, iron and other articles on the dead body. The underlying idea of the Porom-thopthinba ritual is after death the umbilical cord will serve as the path for deliverance. The thread raised in the Porom-thopthinba ritual is called

'Hiri-lang' which serves as guiding line to the abode of the Almighty God. For this reason, after the delivery of the child, the umbilical cord is buried underground with meticulous care. The place where the umbilical cord was buried is considered by the Meities to be the concerned soul's resort or destination or place for worship of the concerned soul. After completion of the disposal of the dead ritual offerings of fruit, arecanut and betel leaf are made at the grave. This is because a spirit comes at the grave every night to stand guard over the departed soul. The offerings are meant for this presiding spirit. The planting of a toon seedling in front of the dead man's head is to enter into communion with mother-earth. This toon is therefore called "malem-leitai-lei".

But, some scholars are of the opinion that, planting of toon seedling was not prevalent at all in the past among the Meiteis and therefore are unwarranted. This practice may have been an imitation of the Hindus planting the basil (Tulasi) behind the dead man's head. They further argue that, for the Meiteis, there was a custom similar to the Kachins of buying funeral grave by offering animal or bird or wine according to their mite. The custom is in vogue by offering a coin in the Meitei society.

There is a concept why a full earthen pot is hung over the grave and water is let fall drop by drop over it by pricking a small hole at the bottom of the pot. The human soul unable to depart the mortal body on account of worldly worries and family ties stays behind. When the dead body is consigned to fire, the soul begins to feel the heat of the burning fire. Even when all the flesh has been fully burnt into ashes, a few bones remain behind to be watched by the soul. To quench the burning sensation of heat felt by the soul, water is made to fall on the grave. The thatched shed on the grave is intended for the departed soul to stay therein until the last death rite is completely performed. The sowing of the seeds on the grave ground is to persuade the soul to stay there. It is an act of coaxing the soul, "Do not bother, when the seeds sprout, once again, you will be reborn in the world". If the seeds grow the soul is supposed to stay calm. If such a soul has ever departed the mortal body as soon as the external winds have blown at the dying moment, it is believed that it will attain deliverance otherwise, the soul stays back watching its mortal remains and bones at the grave. So it is obligatory to undertke the task of watching over the grave and offer oblations there. This offering of oblation with fruits and flowers or cooked rice to the soul is called. 'Taibang-Kaona-hei'.[29] However, nowadays, men well versed in this matter are rare and therefore this ritual practice is being dropped day by day as a superstition. Culture indicates the identity of an ethnic group, so preservation of our culture is much required.

Yumseng-Yummangba.
(Taboos about houses being clean and unclean)

If there is birth or death in a family, the members of the family abstain from religious functions for a specific number of days. The practice is known as Yum-mangba ie the house becomes unclean. Eating of meat and fish is also forbidden in the case of death. The period of the house being unclean is different for birth and death. Different Puyas (Meitei chronicles) specify the time for cleansing the house and mathou-yangenba (Saradha ceremony) differently. The house is cleaned on the tenth or eleventh or twelfth day of death. Eventually, mathou yangenba is performed on the 11th or 12th or 13th day i.e. one day after Yumsengba. At present, Yumsengba is performed on the

12th day and mathouyagenba on the 13th day. The system is basic principles of the Hindus.

The practice of burial is a tradition of the white Miao of South western China. And the practice of cremation and ritualistic materials they used are perhabs influenced by the Vedic Hindus (Hinduism of pre Buddhist and Jaina periods). However, the chanting of rites and rituals are almost the same. Girinni states in his "Ptolemy.s Geography of eastern Asia" that with the decline of the Kalinga power in about second century B.C. Manipur became a Brahmin country. He also described Manipur as the little Brahmin country. The people of this country did not take beef and they could predict the future.[30] There are evidences which can warrant the above views. It may be that the group of people who cremated the dead in the Hindu form might have lost the knowledge of the Hindu rites and rituals and therefore adopted the rites and rituals formerly practised by the people who disposed of the dead by burial with some addition and omission. Those who cremated the dead also performed Nahutpa. (Piercing of ears) and Lugun Thangba (investment of sacred thread) ceremonies like the Hindus. In this respect Jadunath Sarkar remarked that, after the fall of Buddhist Mao-shan (colofen in the 8th century A.D). Manipuries remained as sheep without a spiritual shepherd, just like their Mongoloid Buddhist brothers of Kamarup and Arakan. They had neither learned Brahmin priest nor Buddhist monks. Their worship was almost everywhere conducted by animistic priests.[31]

RITUALS (Lanna thouram) (Ritual ceremony for the salvation of the departed soul)

The soul after departing the mortal body went to the abode of the god either for salvation or re-birth. Deliverance of soul is the main theme of the Meitei religion. To have a right path to heaven and for its deliverance the Meiteis performed many rituals on the eve of departure of the soul and after death. So, they performed elaborate rites and rituals. Viz Leihuntamba.(Astisanchay), 1st Lanna thouram (Sorat or Saradha ceremony) and first death anniversary ritual ceremony (Phiroi or Sabatsarik ceremony). The underlying idea of holding the ceremonies is to repay the debts of the parent by the departed soul. Sorat or Saradha ceremony is use to performed to repay the debt of the father and phiroi is meant for mother.

Though the disposal of the dead the by cremation is different in form from that of the burial, the rites and rituals were similar in many aspects. On the sixth day a procession was made to the grave of the departed soul to perform the ritual of Leihun-tamba. (Offering of the flower to the soul). Nowadays this Leihunlamba is known as "Asthi-loukhatpa" i.e. bringing back of the asthi (a piece of frontal bone) and is performed on a larger scale. For the person whose body was cremated several rituals were performed in successions till the last ceremony of lanna thouram was performed. On the 3rd, 5th and 7th days certain rituals were done.[32] It can't be definitely said whether those who buried the dead observed the ceremony of leihun-tamba. Among the Meo of Thailand after burial an animal sacrifice is made and some of the foods are offered to the soul of the deceased. Additional sacrifices and ceremonies are carried out for three days following the burial and are followed by the festival of the dead one year after the burial as the last oblation. (Leaber etc p.81.). On the 11th or 12th day the house was ritually cleaned (Yum sengaba). The whole house was washed and cleaned up, the earthern cooking pots were broken and thrown out and inmates of the house were also ritually cleansed after washing and bathing. The same practice was also followed by all families of Sagei.(sub-clan)

On the 12thor 13th day the ceremony of "Lanna thouram" was performed.According to Pombilang this Lanna thouram ceremony is called "Mathou Yangenba of the Sun.[33]

In the courtyard of the deceased an owning (Paklei-inlum) is spread and an alter was made for the Almighty God and propitiated, accompanied by the rite of Atai-iratpa.. Then the soul ray of the departed soul is invoked and made to merge with the Supreme God by singing and chanting rites in praise of the deity. On the north east of the awning was planted a post of uchiwa bamboo and on it a long flag is fixed. This flag is called Nongga-Phi. A post of Khoklang tree was also erected to represent the image tree of the deceased person. On the crotch of this tree is placed an earthen saucer on which is spread a white cloth with a red rim. In it are placed a necklace called ngagoi pareng and one whole piece of ginger, complete sets of clothing are laid for both the Kasha ningthou and the departed soul. Flowers and fruits are placed in large heaps. A sumptuous dish of delicious rice and several items of delicacies are displaced. Then, after Kashapaotaklon is sung and Kori tharaochi (copper bugle) blared skywards to intimate the Lai Kasha and a prayer made for the merger of the departed soul with him. The ritual ceremony of kasha paotakpa by erecting a post of khoklang tree is called "Ukrong-hongba". This ceremony was meant for the royal families only.[34] For common people chanting and singing of Kasha-paotaklon was more than enough. Then all the assembled are entertained with a grand feast. For the kiths and kins of departed soul is prepared a family feast and beg for the departed soul to enter into the womb of a virtuous woman in the family or sub clan. This family feast is called "Sagei-Chak-Khangthou".[35]

All these accomplished, the Nungbal Amaiba and the Usha asheiba are offered one cake of salt, nine Chengluk of rice gain, one complete set of clothing and one cow each as largess.[36] This way, the mathou yangenba ceremony of the Sun is performed in full.

Phiroi (1st death anniversary ceremony)

On the completion of one year of a man's death, the last ritual ceremony of deliverance is performed. This ceremony is called Phiroi. This ceremony is performed in order to redeem all the debts the conceived person owes to his mother. One is conceived for ten months by the mother. He/she is in the umbilical placenta as if wrapped up in a cloth, before getting born to this world. In addition to this, the mother suckles him or her for six months, after which she feeds him or her with cooked rice. Thus the parents take care of him or her till one is fully grown to maturity. So, contribution of a parent to a son is beyond our praise. It is said one cannot repay the debts of suckling even one breast of the mother. They (Meiteis) put the position of their parents in a very high status.An adage says "Is the sky high?, Nay, the father is higher, is the earth heavy?, Nay, the mother is heavier".

To repay all this is called Phiroi. To repay the debt of being brought up with food, a feast is offered to God and this offered food is again dedicated to the parents of the dead man concerned. This ritual ceremony of the deliverance is called the mathouyangenba ritual of the moon. As in the previous ceremony, the rituals of Atai-iratpa and Kasha-paotakpa are performed in the occasion of Phiroi. Then all the assembled elders and kiths and kins are entertained with a feast. Thus the aman-singkum ceremony is completed i.e the death ceremony of a man is finished forever. Chronicle like Pombilang warned that, if the process is defective and ever left out, the soul could not get deliverance.[37]

Ukrong-hongba

Though phiroi is the last and final ceremony of death, however, there has been a tradition of offering something or even a grand feast to God on all other death anniversaries. As for the royal families death anniversary was observed every year on a grand scale by way of holding a grand feast accompanied by the ritual of Kasha paotakpa. This annual religious observation of death anniversary was known as Ukrong-hongba. The name owes its origin from the tree (Ukrong) erected for the ritual. Later, from the time of Churachand maharaj of Manipur, this Ukrong-hongba ceremony became known as Ningthem Kritan.

The main theme of the ceremony was, after intimation to lord Kasha by chanting Kasha paotaklon all the assembled people are provided wine and dined to their heart's content. Certain scholars have tried to show Ukrong-hongba as identical with Lanna thouram. But, the philosophical concept of Lanna thouram is totally different from the matter of fact idea of observing Ukrong-hongba. The term Ukrong-hongba itself points out its meaning and purpose. Not only from books but also from archaelogical evidences we can know that both the hillmen and plains people of Manipur performed feast of merit in early days. Nung-hongba, (stone inauguration), U-hongba (tree inauguration), Pukhri-hongba (pond inauguration) etc etc are performed now and then. But the ceremony of Ukhong- hongba was performed by the king or chief only, (relating to kasha -paotaklon) but was forbitten for the common people. There is no evidence of it being observed by common people. The rite of the ceremony itself indicates who would perform it.

Chupsa-moithemba (deliverance of soul for unwanted death)

In the rituals of lanna thouram, the ritual of Chupsa-moithemba is also an unavoidable one, because, unwanted and unnatural death was very common in the then Manipuri society. This ritual is meant for the emancipation of the undelivered soul of a dead man. Death by murder, death from abnoxious deseases, death from falling from the tree, death from drowning in water, death by burning, death on account of child delivery, death by suicide etc. People who suffered unnatural and abnormal deaths were believed to unable to deliverance or salvation of the soul and believed to reoccur the unwanted event to the family or Sagei of the dead man concerned. Such deaths were also believed to cause much hinderence and misfortune to the concerned family or sub-clan. Therefore, Chupsamoithemba is a ritual to pre-empt the reccurence of inauspicious deaths, to deliver the soul of the man who suffered any of the above mentioned inauspicious deaths and for the future well being of the bereaved family or sagei. But there are different opinions when and on which days this ritual should be performed. Probably, it has local variation as Meitei society was formed by different ethinic groups with independent principalities in the early days. In the past this ritual was done on the 4th or 5th or 7th day of the death. But nowadays, this done on the 7th day of the death. If one fails to perform the ritual on these days it should be done well before the Phiroi i.e. the ceremony of first death anniversary. If again, it could not be performed before Phiroi, it ought to be performed on an auspicious day as directed by the expert. The ritual of Chupsa-moithemba has been in vogue since the beginning of the Christian era as a tradition of it having been performed when Nongda lairen Pakhangba was assassinated by his son Khui.[38]

The purpose of CHUPSABA

Chupsaba is synonymous with Chupsa moithemba. The main purposes of this ritual are:-firstly, to lead the undelivered soul to God for salvation, secondly, to protect from diseases and ailments and to pre-empt the recurrence of misfortunes and undesirable accidents or incidents and thirdly, let the affected or distressed family become illustrious and eminent like the splendorous sun shining bright and clear and make it prosperous and affluent and endowed with countless servants and cattle.

There are different forms and methods of Chupsaba and the materials to be used are also different for different forms and methods. Moreover, Chupsaron is very lengthy, systematized and expensive ritualistic affair. Therefore, a simpler and easier form of ritual called Asi-aman-chakkhangba was performed instead. But, nowadays, the majority of the people have abandoned the original traditions and some superstitious person adopted instead the Hinduised forms of rituals which is more convenient to the family.

There are three phases of Chupsaba, 1st emancipation of the undelivered soul by guiding it to the Almighty God is the main item of the ritual, 2nd to cleanse the house of the affected family and then cleanse the surviving members of the family from nightmares, incurable diseases and ailmens and recurrence of inauspicious incidents or incidence of the past. Srdly and lastly a ritual ceremony called phungathongba (laying of hearth) is observed. After laying a new fireplace, rice and curry is cooked under certain prescribed rules as in the ancestor worship and offered to the Almighty God and goddess Imoinu. Then all the members of the family with or without the members of the sagei will hold a feast with a prayer to god for prosperity, well being and ascendancy in power and status. When everything is over, some food offered to God will be laid outside the homestead to shut the gate of death at the grave.

This ritual of Chupsaba shall be performed in the morning. All the members of the .household are compulsory to participate in it but participation of the members of the Sagei is optional.

Asi-aman Chakkhangba (feasting of the departed soul)

This ritual is another version of Chups-amoithemba. Whenever there is recurrence of unnatural and abnormal deaths in the family and if obstacles and hinderences happened in that family and if that family ever failed to perform Chupsaba of an unwanted death in the family, the ritual of Asi-aman chakkhangba is performed in place of Chupsa moithemba.

The ritual is less expensive, far shorter and less time consuming. Many of the restrictions in the Chupsaba are relaxed in it. So in order to save time and money, Asi-aman chakkhangba was performed in lieu of chupsa-moithemba. In this ritual, after all essential articles and materials are displayed, the rites of anam-athou, Yumdai-naksang and Iru-laishol are chanted to cleanse and sanctify the house, its inmates and all the people persent then and there. Then, Atai-laisol, maikei-ngakpa-laiyam taiba, pongning, Tamna shitpa, tutenglon and Numitkappa are recited and chanted so as to lead the undelivered soul of the man who died an unnatural death to the Supreme God for salvation. The soul which could not attain deliverance would be able to get emancipation at last.

All the food items employed in this ritual including rice and vegetables can be cooked and partaken of. From a dish made of the cooked food, separate portions are laid outside the house compound for nine Laibungthous (nine gods), seven Lainuras (seven goddesses) and sixtyone sarois (61 evil spirits). Seven lines are drown there, to shut the door or path with due ritual.[39]

Lanchak-khangba. (Deliverance of the war victims)

The souls of the people who died in battle and hunting (mainly in battle) are believed to be unable to get deliverance. Such undelivered souls often visit the village where the war was fought or the enemy who killed them. They gave obstacles, hindrances and terror to the villagers and the enemy concerned and his household. The ritual performed to ward off such obstruction and to deliver the vindictive souls is known as Lanchak-khangba. Lanchak-khangba is done for the troubled family or for the whole village or for the entire country according to its degree or nature of obstruction. For this ritual, on an auspicious day food is cooked at naktha (left side of the varenda). In a winnowing basket called Yangkok are placed seven dishes of the cooked food, seven flags of seven colour are spread from north to south with white first and black last, seven wax lamps, seven sets of fruits and seven coins. The winnowing basket is carried from the naktha (left side of the porch) to the grave of a man who died on Saturday or to the extremity of the village where the customary ritual chanting and worship is done. The undelivered soul is given its due share of the food and is let to merge with the Almighty God or driven out i.e. exorcised. Then, the ritual shutting of the door of death (Mangthong Thingba) will be performed. The priest who performs this ritual will spell out the names of the war victims. He himself will be in the dress of an army, black-cloths, a spear and a sword in hands and behave in a soldierly manner.[40]

Lai-amangba (unclean spirits)

In the salvation ritual for the un-emancipated souls or spirits, mention may be made of Lai-amangba commonly known as Soren (a type of poltergeist) having three different types viz, Apumbi (a foetus expelled prematurely from the womb), Soren (a child born dead after recurrent birth and death or a child who dies before three years of age) and Kasha (spirits of those children who have died without having known their parents or the people who have died in the wilderness unknown and undiscovered). Spirits or souls of suchuperson are believed not able to get the deliverance. Unable to return human world (rebirth) or go to the divine world, they remain ever hovering in the sky. It is believed that, these spirits undergo recurrent births and cause obstruction and hindrances in several homes.

They cause consternation, illness and sickness, impairment of the body and soul, extravagant wastage of money and other inconveniences. They often go to the compound where they once dwelt or to the house where they to took birth or to their grave. Sometime these evil spirits are employed for witchcraft and sent to the house of a man by his ill-wisher.They may also follow a man who has accidentally trespassed their habitat. They may also venture into a house of a certain man the moment when they desire to have their food. In short they are the most dangerous group of evil spirits to harass mankind.

There was no tradition of performing any ritual ceremony of for the salvation of such spirits. It was done only when they resorted to perpetration of hindrances and obstructions. It is believed that such obstructions and hindrances can be avoided if a kind of ritual called Soren Shorat is performed on the completion of three months of the death. As and when they perpetrate obstructions and hindrances, with the help of experts, they can be driven out, emancipated and if intransigent, kept in captivity. For every type of Soren, the procedures and rituals are different. By offering food and cloths to the spirit, the expert carries out the ritual function on an unauspicious day of a particular month during the night.

The role of Maiba in the death ceremony

The expert who attend the last moment of the dying person is known as Maiba. Similar name is also given to the expert who performed the death rituals. The term maiba is synonymous with Amaiba. The former became known as Beita (Vaida) and the second one as purohit by the Hindunised Meiteis. A systematic form of death ritual began to be performed in the land from the 2nd era i.e. Hayachak, by the time a priest from east Bengal (Pasha) called Urok played the role of the preist. In the 3rd era it was substituted by Nongpal amaiba experts from the Angom clan which was followed by Nungpal amaiba. (amaiba from the Luwang clan) in the last era i.e. Konna-chak.

Maiba plays a great role in the death ceremony. From the last moment of the dying person upto the end of the salvation death ceremony, the maiba performs many functions. In relation to death ceremony, the maiba may be broadly divided into two types, namely, the maiba who performs rituals at salvation ceremony (Lanna thouram). The maiba who accompanies the dead body is now called the

Baita (Vaida). Since the Meiteis have embraced Hinduism, the maiba for the salvation ceremony has been replaced by Brahmin Purohit. Even the baita also has been played by a Brahmin.. When the illness of a patient is at its critical juncture, a maiba is engaged to attend him. The dying man will at first begin breathing with rhythm by jerking his chin and moving lips (khadang inba). Then if he starts breathing at a faster rythms with his elbow pulling up, this is called the uprooting of life soul (Brahma-phukpa). By this time a bedding will be arranged at lapyan ka (the room in the south east corner of the house). Nowadays it is done in the porch. At this juncture the maiba will do everything to enable the dying man to go to the abode of God in the right path. The ritual of shutting and opening of the nine doors of the mortal body is to be made. The passage should be made in the three spots viz, navel, crown of the head and the space between the two eyebrows. The last one is believed to be the best place. If the soul spirit ever left the mortal body in this passage, the soul got its deliverance i.e. got salvation otherwise, until the dead body is carried to the Yathok shang the maiba will detain the vestige of Brahma (soul) of the dying man by placing his palm on the navel of the dying man. When the soul has left the mortal body, the maiba will do all the ritual functions required for the disposal of the dead body i.e the last oblation to the departed soul. In some cases, such ritual is entrusted to another maiba who knows well the formality of lanna thouram. Then he will make a ritual shout to set out for thr funeral ground. Nowadays, the ritual shouting has been replaced by Brindavan yatra by the Hindunised Meiteis. In the early days, when the dead body has been inside the yathoksang, the maiba shall no longer perform anything. He should hold tight the remaining part of the soul in the body of the dying man (brahma teja) by clenching his right fist tight. The remaining part of the body is brought to the funeral ground. The maiba will hold jointly the knife of the grave watcher or Kira performer (person who performs the funeral oblation) and entrust to it the remaninig part of the soul.

On the day of 1st Lanna thouram or Shorat (Shardha), the maiba will enter the Sankritan arena during the Shambhuk (Sambhog), at the culmination of the ceremony and touch the drums and Cymbals so as to entrust the remaining part of soul to the Almighty God. Some are of the opinion that by the time as mentioned above the maiba carried with him the departed soul inside the arena of the Sanskritan and entrusted to the Almighty God for deliverance. So, the role of the maiba in the disposal of the dead specially for the deliverance of the departed soul is very great. All these rituals are meant for the cremated group

The seat of the maiba in the death ceremony

On the lanna thouram day a special seat arrangement must be made for the maiba. The seat for the maiba is made at one of the three places under the Illum-paklei (temporary pavilion). The three places are, 1) south east corner 2) northeast corner and 3) near the conch shell blower. The seating is different according to the age of the deceased person concerned. If the ceremony is meant for an unmarried youngman or woman or a child, the maiba will sit in southeast. For senior people, the seat must be in the north east. But in the present day regardless of the norms, the seat is arranged in the south east corner, in the 1st row. Sometimes, if there was inconvinences to arrange the seat under norm, the seat may be placed near the conch blower. The maiba who acts as beita should be pleased by giving cloths and largesse. The maiba attends the dying man till death by standing watch and ward without any sleep. Yet, he is bound by tradition not to accept any remuneration or largesse for his services until the day of lanna thouram.

Rules for erecting YATHOKSHANG

Erection of Yathokshang (temporary makeshift for dead body) was done under certain fixed rules. The shed is erected at Khangenpham. (The space for laying the dead body in the courtyard) opposite to Brindadevi (if ever planted) but a little ahead. If the space does not permit, it can be done along the Brindadevi in the south. For the aged and people ordained as Sanyasis, the foundation pillar is erected opposite to the Yengai-sangjin (southern extremity of the loft in the front of the house where the chickens were kept). If, however the ridge of the house is north to south or if space does not permit, the foundation of the pillar will be done opposite to the southern jamb of the main door. The foundation starts from southeast, ends in the north west. In the case of youngman and girls, the Yathoksang will be set up opposite the point three fingers away from the ridge of the house and the foundation pillar will be laid on the southeast. As soon as the dead body is carried to the funeral ground, the shed is be dismantled and brought to the funeral ground to be burnt there. If the ritual of mangthong thingba is desired, the maiba may perform the same at the time of dismantlement of the Yathoksang. He will intone the ritual incantation and push the shed outwards.

Shinglup (death organization)

There has been a tradition in the Meitei society since the early time to extend assistance to the bereaved family by way of forming an organization called shinglup or shingyenglup confined in the locality or leikai, for looking after a dying person and rendering help in the death ceremony. Singlup = Shing+lup. Shing = firewood and lup

= organization or association. So, it meant organization for supplying firewood at the cremation of the death body. In strict sense, it is a dead organization. Such organizations are formed in the locality according to the local convenience or advantage. All the local residents within the jurisdication of the organization shall be its members. The system is in vogue till now. In the early days those who failed to pay the fee for mangkat at the time of marriage were not allowed to perform cremation or burial in the village cremation or burial ground. Similarly, outsiders or strangers were not admitted. The elders of the locality will guide and manage the death organization and conduct all the relevant affairs by bidding the younger generation. When a person is on the verge of death, all the members will, in turn stand watch and ward over the patient by lighting a fire. (Meilingba). The members of the shinglup will render help in the disposal of the dead on the day of death and also in the lanna thouram. One member each of every household will comeout to participate in the disposal of dead, erection of the pavilion for the lanna thouram ceremony and clearing of the adjoining area. In early days each and every household would bring a fuel log as a contribution towards the cremation of the dead body. From this act of contributing firelog (shing) the name shinglup was so named. Every household used to grow for firewood, easily combustible trees like heikreng in the household compound. But nowadays, instead of contributing firewood, monetary contribution of a fixed amount to meet the expenses of firewood has become the order of the day. At the same time the early system of meilingba to stand watch and ward over the dying person began to be dropped. Even the essence and meaning Shinglup are forgotten and unobserved. Though, we find an image of a well organised society with mutual cooperation and help in the early Meitei society, it is fast changing in the late 20th century leading to an individualistic western society.

REFERENCES

1. N. Manijao - Pombilang. p. 25.
2. Ariba Meitei-Laining lichat (Manipuri chronicle), pp. 136-141 P.c.
3. N. Ibochouba-Thirel layat. p. 25.
4. Singtabung(U.Ch) - last part.
5. Ng. Kulachandra- Apokpa thouniron. p. 10.
6. Ibohal and Rajen - Sakok lamlen. p. 30.
7. N. Ibochouba. Thirel layat. p. 25 &Maputhiba (unpublished chronicle).
8. Y. Bhagya. Leithak leikharol. p. 55.
9. N. Manijao : opcit. p. 3.
10. N. Ibochouba-opcit. p. 24..
11. Ibid. p. 25.
12. Khamoi yamoi. (U.Ch). p. 5.
13. Ch. Joy. Malem Leishemlon Ariba Vol: II, p. 193.
14. M. Narendra. Lang-ol. p. 44.
15. Ariba Meitei laining lichat. (U.Ch). p. 87(pc).
16. Garbha bichar. (U.Ch). p. 3-4..
17. Ibid. p. 5.
18. M. Chandra Singh. Panthoibi Khongul. p. 71
19. Ch. Joy-opcit. p. 192
20. Ibohal and Rajen opcit. p. 8
21 Frank M. Lebar, Gerald C. Hickey,& John K.Musgrave :- Ethinic groups of mainland southeast Asia. p. 72
22. M. Chandrasekhar. Loiyumba silyen. p. 81-82
23. Puroi-masin- (U.Ch) Latam.
24. M. Gourachandra :- Thouwanthaba hiran. pp. 36-283
25. Rev. Sidney Endle :- The Kacharis. pp. 47-48
26. Ch. Joy. Opcit. p. 193.

27. Ch. Joy- opcit. p. 194.
28. Thougan mashin. (U.Ch). p. 11
29. Shilthong lamlen- (U.Ch)- P.c
30 G.E. Gerinni- Researches on Ptolemy's Geography of Eastern Asia. p. 33
31. Jadunath Sarkar- The history of Bengal, p. 227.
32. Y. Budhimacha- Thaloi-nongkhailon. p. 58.
33. Ng. Manijao - opcit. p. 39.
34 Ni.Khelchandra :- Naothingkhong Phambal Kaba. p. 79, Kh. Yaima- Anoiron Vol I, p. 4 and Ibohal & Rajen — opcit. p. 8.
35. Ch. Joy opcit. p. 93
36. Ibohal & Rajen opcit. p. 9
37. Ng. Manijao. Opcit. p. 38.
38. Chuparon mapal- (U.Ch).
39. Asi-amn chak khangba- (U.Ch)
40. Madhop and Khelehandra: U.Ch=unpublished chronicle. Khunung lichat shajat. p. 64.

CHAPTER FIVE

CONCLUSION

The Meiteis have a high philosophy about birth and death. Not only they know about the after world, the concept of soul is an interesting aspect for discussion. Under their beliefs, human life on this earth is caused by Almighty God, creator of this universe. It is generally believed that the soul is an image of the supreme god and passing through different natural phenomena one after another, enters the maternal womb. The sperm after passing through six objects came to father and carrying it for two months father passes to the mother and finally the mother conceives it for ten months in the womb and the child is born.

To beget a good child wiseman observed certain norms of co-habitation and to avoid any obstruction and problem in the delivery certain rituals were performed in different months during the period of pregnancy. They did not know the modern science, yet they took special care for the delivery of the child and health of the mother. The delivery was usually done in their own house, assisted by local experts, Chabokpi-maibai and an assistant, maiyoknabi. Just after the birth of the child the father gave the name of the god to the newly born child. They took due care for umbilical cord and it was buried on the side of the house with due rituals. At the sametime, due care was also taken for the mother by keeping her in a separate room near the hearth of the house giving separate and restricted food items. On the 10th or 11th day of the birth, on the day of Yumsengba medication was done to the mother for her health. So, we find some sort of hygienic method in their child birth.

The birth of a child was celebrated with a ritual called "Ipan". The ritual is devided into two parts, morning item and evening item having equal degree. Hindunisation brought certain changes in the rituals. The morning item was substituted for Hindu ritual of Swasti Pijah. Nowadays, some revivalist section has altogether dropped Hindu ritual and once more revived traditional practices but partially which is not in conformity with what are written in their chronicles.

The next aspect of their life circle ceremony is naming of the child. No specific rite and ritual was there for the naming of the child though it is considered compulsory. Probably, it was in the form decleration. The naming is to be made after Ipan. The present style of naming came into existence after Hindunisation. Early form too can be divided into two stages i.e pre formation and post formation period of Yek and Salai.

The third ceremony is 'Cha-umba' i.e. food giving ceremony to the child. A baby become acquitant to take solid form of food after few a months. So the ritual of Chaumba use to performed when the baby became three month old. But boys are not taking much interest in taking the solid form of food for a longer period. So, for them it was usually held in the 5th month. The ceremony of Chaumba was held with due rituals accompanied by an omen seeking under an expert.

Na-hutpa i.e. ear boring ceremony formed the 4th one in their life circle ceremony. The main purpose of the ceremony was for the longevity of the childs' life and to protect from the evil spirits. Again there was a tradition that if a child dies before earboring they (Meities) used to performed reverse system in the disposal of dead and proper norms of death rituals were forbidden. So, from religious points of view ear boring was an unavoidable and compulsory custom among the Meities.

The next item of their life circle ceremony is Lugun - thangba (Investment of secred threads). From time immorial a section of the Meities got the influence of Hinduism and practised Hindu ritual viz investment of sacred threads (upanayan) and cremation of dead body in Hindu model. But here investment of some sacred threads was forbidden to each and every person. Only piba, the head of the Sagei was invested with the Lugun. Again, unlike the Hindus the Lugun was tied to the hair knot instead of keeping it over the shoulder.

The Meiteis took special care for the education of their children. As there was no formal educational institutions, they sent their children to the house of the experts. As soon as the children got the age of women in the evening and learned the arts of spinning, weaving, embroidery, song, dance, Yumbalon etc. Similarly, the boys got the training of different arts including the art of warfare from different experts. Though we can not get any authentic records in this respect, it is comparable with Hindu system of Vidyaarambha under Gurukul system with some local variation. The kabui tribe of Manipur which has close affinity with the Meitei started the education of their children with due ceremony and kept the children in dormitory. But the system of dormitony was not prevalent among the Meities.

Another important aspect of the life circle ceremony of the Meiteis is marriage. The tie for husband and wife required a solemnization by a ritual viz, Luhongba, Keinya katpa and Loukhatpa. Early system of their marriage was the prototype of the southern Tais with some local variation. But it was a gradual development, adding new elements throughout the ages leading to the formation of the present system. In reality, the present system is the outcome of the Hindunisation in the 18th century A.D. But we can find heritage of the past in tact and the new flavour of Hindunisation can easily be separated.

In the early times marriage age was 16-18 for boys and 13-15 yrs for girls. Elopment (Gandharava bibah) was the most common and favourite form of marriage though engagement or go-between was considered an ideal. Whatever the system of becoming husband and wife i.e chenba or chingba a solemnization either by Keinya katpa or Loukhatpa or marriage with restricted ritual was made. In rare cases, the guardian refuge to recognize the union. Such partners and their children were not only looked down upon but also certain social restrictions were imposed.

Monogamy was the common feature, but the chiefs and well-to- do persons adopted polygamy. At the sametime, before the Christian era there was the heritage of Polyandry, but at present there is no trace of it. Regarding the marriage rules, the Meiteis are exogamous. The rule of matrimonial alliance was based on both patrilineal and matrilineal kinship system side by side. But they began to neglect their customs from the 2nd half of the last quarter of the 20th century A.D. Taking of the bride price and giving of limited dowry was prevalent among the Meiteis which was an important feature of the Muru or Lawang tribe. But taking of bride price is completely dropped in the heart of the Imphal town as a disgraceful system. Thanks to god unlike the Hindus of mainland India there is no problems of dowry and birth of the female child in the valley.

Betrothal ceremony is a very lengthy and costly process. But the early system was to some extent shorter then the present system. In the early Christian era garlanding of the couple before the members present was the form of marriage. The system of Kujaba punba and Kujaba was a later addition probably from the 17th century A.D. Then the custom of Leikoiba was again added in the 18th centuryA.D. So, we find a gradual development adding new elements in their marriage system. The marriage system of the Loi-communities in the valley differs from the Meiteis though there are some point of similarity. Similarly, there are many points of similarity between the Meiteis, Tangkhul and Kuki tribes of Manipur. It is safe to conclude that, the marriage system of the Meiteis is synthesis of the tribal culture with Tai culture, to which a new flavour of Hinduism was added.

The last important aspect of their life circle ceremony is the disposal of the dead and its related ceremonies. They performed different forms in the disposal of the dead in different eras. In the 1st era (Hayi-chak) the dead body was disposed in the air and water (kept a few days in open air and then thrown in the water) In the next era (Haya-chak) it was buried. But in the 3rd era (Langba-chak) there were two systems of disposal of the dead i.e. burial and cremation side by side by different groups. The system continued in the last era (Konachak) until and unless they were converted in Hindunism. After Hindunisation cremation became a common feature through out the whole valley regardless of the local tribes. Till now, the local tribes perform burial.

Though, the Meiteis believe in the laws of Nature, they attributed different factors to the death of a person. So, they performed many rituals to ward off untimely death. Under this belief, the soul spirit left the mortal body and went to the abode of the Almighty God. The soul of the dying person was lured by the goddess of death called Khamnung keikaoi louonbi and was left the soul in the land of death. The main theme of the Meitei religion was deliverance of soul i.e. to unite with the supreme diety or rebirth. Rebirth was also considered as deliverance of soul. One who could not get deliverance but awaiting the favour of the Almighty God lived together with their ancestors in heaven. But other are in the status of demi God. If the soul spirit is to be reborn, it passes through different natural objects and live for a considerable periods before rebirth. But one may be reborn in the mortal life on the very day of one's death. But such cases are exceptional and it is believed that the soul spirit got its deliverance. Thus we find two concepts in the deliverance of the soul viz, to unite with the Almighty god (Mukti or Nirvana) and rebirth. Like the Hindus, Meiteis also believed in the concept of heaven after death while the wrong doers went to the hell. Under their belief there are three heavens viz. 1) Koubru hill. 2) Seloi-langmai hill and 3)Thangjing hill. Seloi-langmai hill alias Tarang Ching is regarded as the abode of Atiya kuru sidaba. His abode is known as Konkhei-atamba. The place may be treated as the top of the three heaven but their chroicles like, Pudin, Leithak Leikharol and Yabirok describe Koubru hill as the top of the Heaven. So, they have high philosophical idea about soul which is peculiar to Hindu concept with local variation and tribal ideas.

During our periods of study, the Meiteis performed two types of disposal of the dead. 1) Burial and 2) Cremation as stated above. Though most of the social Anthropologists unanimously pointed out that, the Meiteis are offshoot of the local tribes or have common origin, but the nature of disposal of the dead was different. Unlike the local tribes they practiced primary and secondary burial. They exhumed the dead body after one year and such culture is found among the Meo tribe of southern Szechwan in China. Again the nature of cremation may be identified as Vedic culture of pre-Biddhist and pre Jaina periods. Thus the system is also comparable with that of the Riang of Chitangong and Bodo Kacharis of Assam. So, we find different aspects of culture in their life circle ceremony.

Elaborate rituals were perfomed for the disposal of the dead and deliverance of the departed soul, which they called Mathou yangenba. For a complete one year many rituals used to be performed at interval, such rituals were very expensive and time consuming. The main theme of the rituals is to send off the departed soul through a right way on which it come from and reunite with the Almighty god. Again, for the deliverance of the soul who died unnatural, ugly death and for uncleaned spirits some specific rituals were performed.

BIBLIOGRAPHY

Primary sources
Meitei chronicles not yet published,(U.CH)

1) Ariba laining lichat.
2) Asi-aman-chak khangba.
3) Anouba-Pen-teenaba.
4) Angom Khonghou-Khoira.
5) Chupsharon (two different chronicles)
6) Cha-umlon.
7) Chakpa Khunda Khunthoklon.
8) Garbha-bichar
9) Ipanthaba.
10) Itinaba & Pentinaba.
11) Khununglen
12) Khamoi-yamoi.
13) Kasha-paotaklon
14) Karathong lamlen.
15) Keiroi
16) Khagemba Yumlep.
17) Khundaron.
18) Kei loi lingkhatpa.
19) Lai Khunda.
20) Langdai langhei.
21) Leimarel Sekning.

22) Miyat
23) Maputhiba-alia Soupol-Yairel chanu.
24) Meihourol Shakok.
25) Ningthourol Shingkak.
26) Nonggaron.
27) Pombirol.
28) Puwari
29) Puroi mashin. (two different puyas)
30) Singdabung (Kyan)
31) Shilthong lamlel.
32) Sanamahi laihui.
33) Thouniron.
34) Thougal mashin.
35) Heirem Puwari

Published Chronicles.

C.H. Nganba (Joy):- *Malem leishemlol Ariba.* vol II. Imphal-1994.

I. Amubi Singh :- *Leihou-naophamlon.* Imphal-1981.

Kh. Yaima Singh 1) *Poireiton Khunthokpa.* Imphall971.

Kh. Chandrasekhar Singh :- *Loiyumba Shinyel.* Imphal 1975.

Ibohal and Rajen - *Shakok Lamlen.* Imphal 1973.

M. Gourachandra Singh :- 1) *Thouwanthaba Hiran.* Kakching 1978. 2) *Khamlang Puwari Ahuiron.* Kakching-1977.

M. Chandra Singh :- *Panthoibi Khongul.* Imphal 1972 (2nd ed).

Manipur state kala Academy. *Sagei Salairon.* Imphal 1994. Mangi-*Chakparon.*

N. Manijao- *Pornbilang.* Imphal-1972 (2nd sd)

N. Naran- *Nonglon Pathup Wakhetlon.* Imphal 1983.

N. Khelchandra Singh. 1) *Chinggoiron.* Imphal 1983. 2) Chothe thangwai pakhangba & Nongpan pombi luwaoba. Imphal 1980. 3) Naothingkhong Phambal kaba.Imphal 1967. 4) Khuman kangleiron. Imphal 5) Phamlon. Imphal 1987. N. Indramani Singh- *Pakhangba laihui.* Imphal 1981.

N. Ibochouba Singh 1) *Thirel layat.* Imphal 1981. 2) Thirel meiramliba . Imp.

N. Amuyaima :- *Panthoibi Naherol and Aman Singkum Ion.*

Imphal 1997.

Y. Budhichandra : *Thaloi nongkhailon.* Imphal 1986.

Y. Bhagya : Leithak laikharon. Imphal 1994 (3rd Edn).

Secondary sources.
(Manipuri section)

A. Chiteswar Sharma :- *Meiteigi hongnemba and Ukrong Hongba.* Imphal 2003.

B. Kulachandra Sharma :- *Meiteigi Luhongba & Louna*

Leinabagi Welel Wakhul. Imphal 1998. Ch. Nganba(Joy). *Aman Shingkumlon Thouram.* Imphal 1992.

S. Nilabir :- *Irat Thouram.* Imphal 2004.

Kala :- *Chingu Nongdamba.* Imphal 1985.

Kh. Yaima Singh-Ariba Shinthong. Imphal 1988.

Kh. Chandrasekhar Singh :- *Irat laishol.* Imphal 1984.

Kh. Yaima :- Meitei Jagoi Vol I. Imphal 1973.

M. Ibotombi- *Irat thouniron.* Imphal 1977.

M. Narendra :- *langwon.* Imphal 1981.

Madhab & Khelchandra. *Khumnung Lichat shajat.* Imphal 1970.

N. Birachandra. *Early Settlement and Early Names on Manipur.* Imphal 1993.

Ng. Kulachandra Singh. *Apokpa Thouniron.* Imphal 1967.

Sobita Devi:- *Moirang Kangleiron.* Imphal 1982.

Y. Tolchousana :- *Meitei Lairik Mathang.* Imphal 1970.

Y. Tamphajao :- *Meitei Thouramgi Wangnlon.* Imphal 1992.

L. Mangi & L. Mani Singh :- *Meitei Puran (Garibaniwaj Charitra).* Imphal 1969.

English Section

A.R. Colqhoun :- *Ethinic history of the Shan.* Delhi-1985.

Bertrams, Carry and H.N. Tuck :- *The Chin hills,* vol I & II Calcutta 1976.

B.J. Terwiel:- *The Tai of Assam and ancient Tai ritual* vol I & II.Gaya - 1980.

C. Gilhodes :- *TheKachins (Religion & Culture)* New Delhi 1995.

Girinni :- *Reaserches on Ptolemy geography of Eastern Asia.* London 1974.

G.H. Luce :- *Phases of Pre-pagan. Burma,* vol I. London 1985.

Gogoi. P :- *The Tai and Tai Kingdom-* Gauhati-1968. H

elmut Hoffmoun :- (Translated by Eward Fizerad) *The Religion of Tibet.* London-1962.

Jadunath Sarkar :- *The History of Bengal* (Muslim Period) Delhi-1977.

Kapadia.Km. :- *Marriage and Family in India.* Calcutta 1979.

Miller A.U. Hegel's *Phenomenology of Spirit.* Oxford-1979.

N.K. Kadetoted :- *Family and Marriage.* Delhi-1979.

Patricia Uberoi :- *Family, Kinship and Marriage in India.* New Delhi-1993.

Regional-le-may :- *The culture of South east Asia.* N. Delhi 1962.

Rev. Sidney Endle :- *The Kacharis.* Delhi-1997.

R. Brown :- *Statitical account of Manipur and the Hill Territories Under its Rule.* Cal-1974.

Savadaman Singh- *Polyandry in ancient India.* Lucknow-1978.

T.C. Hudson. *The Meithei.* Delhi 1975.

V.V.Prakasa Rao & V. Nandini Rao :- *Marriage, the Family and Women in India.* New Delhi-1985.

Wallis Budge E.A. *The Egyptian Book of Death.* New York 1978.

Tertiary Sources

Manipur State Archrive Imphal-collected Seminar Paper vol. IV Imp-2003.

Ch. Budhi Singh:- Major marriage Rules of the Meiteis (paper presented in the seminar orgn by N.E. India Historical Society Held in Imphal.

Bulletin of the Dept of Anthropology Govt of India. Cal-1955 Cult of Dead and Funery Custom of the Riang by Bhupendra Mukherjee.

Asiatic society of Bengal :- Major C.M. Enriquer- Story of Migrations.

A Report on the Excavation of Sekta : O.Kumar Singh. Imphal 1994 published by state Archaeology of Manipur.

INDEX

□□□